THINGS THAT AREN'T SO

THINGS THAT AREN'T SO

BY DR. R. B. OUELLETTE

SWORD of the LORD PUBLISHERS

Post Office Box 1099 • Murfreesboro, Tennessee 37133

Sword of the Lord Publishers
ISBN 0-87398-888-9

All Scripture quotations are from
the King James Bible.

Printed and Bound in the United States of America

CONTENTS

CHAPTER ONE
IS BURNOUT A REAL DANGER?

Not too long ago, I had a problem with one of my knees. I had arthroscopic surgery on it back in the eighties, and it started giving me trouble again. I went to my regular doctor, and he sent me to a specialist. The specialist did several tests to see how bad the problem was.

He showed me some X-rays. He said, "These are the knees of a seventy-year-old man." Then he showed me the X-rays of my knees. "Yours are worse," he said. "You're ready for a knee replacement. Your knees are just worn out." After we discussed my situation, we decided that I would wait a while longer before having my knees replaced.

That got me to thinking about the topic of burnout. It's something we hear a lot about today. There's a great deal of focus on the danger of falling prey to overwork and stress, but is that a legitimate concern?

I can't stop my body from getting older, but I can keep from having the attitude that I'm old. One does not get old unless his mind tells him he is old. I only have one life to serve God, and I want to make the most of it. I had a lady on our church staff do some research, and she found out that in the 1930s, the average work-week was eighteen hours longer than it is today—and we think we're overworked!

THE COMMON TEACHING

It is commonly taught that Christians are overworked, overstressed and in danger of burnout.

Twenty-first-century Christians, we often hear, are overworked,

1

overstressed and in danger of burnout. People say, "It's just so hard in this day and age. We have more pressure, stress and difficulty than ever before. Watch out for burnout."

It's almost impossible to listen to Christian radio or television for any length of time without hearing about the danger of burnout. I was listening to a couple of Christian psychologists one day on the radio talking about people they referred to as "pleasers." They said this kind of person always says yes and does too much and that he needs to learn how to say no.

What was intriguing to me was that a lady called up the program and complained about how busy she was. She talked about all the commitments she had and how she was stretched too thin. Her solution was to drop all the things she was doing at the church. She kept the PTA and the Red Cross and Neighborhood Watch.

If you have to give up something, don't give up something of eternal value. Those Christian psychologists didn't seem to see anything wrong with her solution. They didn't suggest to her that the eternal was more important than the temporal and should have priority.

Jesus told the disciples to come apart and rest for a while.

The proponents of this teaching say that if you don't come apart and rest, you'll come apart.

Before I started traveling and preaching, I took a day off almost every week. If I'm going somewhere to preach that my family would enjoy and if our schedule allows it, I take them with me. I take two weeks' vacation every year. I'm not against rest.

This common teaching on burnout, however, does not match what the Bible says. In fact, by looking at Mark 6, the context of this verse that is so often used to warn of burnout, we find a very different truth from what is commonly taught.

THE CONTRADICTORY TRUTH

The disciples were tired.

"And the apostles gathered themselves together unto Jesus, and told him all things, both what they had done, and what they had taught.

"And he said unto them, Come ye yourselves apart into a desert place, and rest a while: for there were many coming and going, and they had no leisure so much as to eat."—Mark 6:30, 31.

Jesus sent the disciples out two by two to go throughout the countryside and preach the Gospel (vss. 7–13). People responded to the message. The Bible says the disciples were so busy, they did not have time to eat. If most of us are honest, we admit there aren't very many times we're too busy to eat. Eating holds a pretty high priority! When the disciples were tired and worn out, Jesus said they needed to rest.

Jesus took them to a desert place.

Mark 6:32 says, "And they departed into a desert place by ship privately." They needed a day off. Yet the Bible says that the people followed the ship on foot when they saw Jesus leaving. One of the things that we sometimes overlook in Scripture is the tremendous appeal Jesus had to common people. They would go to great lengths to see and hear Him.

The Sea of Galilee is eight miles wide and thirteen miles long. In the day of Christ, there were nine towns around it. None of them had a population of fewer than 15,000. What happened was that, as those who witnessed Jesus and the disciples' leaving made their way around the lake, people from those cities joined them so they could also hear Jesus.

When Jesus got off the boat, He saw "much people." I think it's reasonable to assume there were 20,000 or more people there to hear Him, based on the fact that we are told there were 5,000 men. Without any advertisement or promotion, word of mouth gathered a huge crowd.

Jesus taught the multitude all day.

The day that was to have been devoted to resting was devoted to ministry instead. All day long, Jesus taught the people. Finally, the disciples came to Jesus and said, "The time is far passed" (Mark 6:37). When they protested, saying they didn't have enough money for the task, Jesus asked them what they did have.

It's interesting to me how He focused on what they did have rather than what they lacked. You can always complain about a lack of time or energy to accomplish a task. Instead of doing that, use what you do have. God multiplies what we have when we give it to Him. I wonder sometimes how many blessings and miracles we miss out on by giving up because we're tired.

The disciples fed the hungry crowd.

After Jesus determined that they had five loaves and two fish, He issued instructions to the disciples. They first divided the people into groups. Then the disciples served the food to them. Finally, when everyone had eaten all he wanted, the disciples gathered up what was left over.

If our estimate that there were 20,000 people in the crowd is correct, each disciple would have needed to take food to around 1,700 people. I believe the disciples were more tired at the end of the day than they were at the beginning of the day. That was the final result of their day to relax, when they 'came apart to rest.'

The Bible tells us that there were twelve baskets of food left over—one for each of the disciples but none for Jesus. Never during His life on earth did Jesus use His divine power for personal benefit. Instead, He went to refresh His strength in prayer.

The disciples then went back across the lake while Jesus stayed to pray.

"And straightway he constrained his disciples to get into the ship, and to go to the other side before unto Bethsaida, while he sent away the people.

"And when he had sent them away, he departed into a mountain to pray."—Mark 6:45, 46.

Jesus was just as physically tired as the disciples, if not more so. He had undoubtedly needed a day of rest just as much as they had. All day long He had taught the multitude of people who gathered to hear Him. Working miracles exacted a physical toll on Jesus (Mark 5:30).

Yet rather than taking the night to sleep, He took the night to pray. As we'll see in the conclusion, many of the problems we attribute to burnout are caused by depending on our own strength rather than relying on divine power to accomplish the tasks that God has set before us.

4

A storm prevented the disciples from returning until Jesus calmed the sea.

Jesus interrupted His praying to come to the disciples and rescue them from the storm. Mark 6:48 says, "And he saw them toiling in rowing; for the wind was contrary unto them: and about the fourth watch of the night he cometh unto them, walking upon the sea, and would have passed by them."

The fourth watch was getting close to morning, so the hard physical work of the disciples had continued for most of the night. Finally, when Jesus came into the ship, the storm ceased. Mark 6:51 says, "And he went up unto them into the ship; and the wind ceased: and they were sore amazed in themselves beyond measure, and wondered."

After no rest, no sleep, no break in their schedule and after having toiled all night, they started all over again the next day.

"And when they were come out of the ship, straightway they knew him,

"And ran through that whole region round about, and began to carry about in beds those that were sick, where they heard he was.

"And whithersoever he entered, into villages, or cities, or country, they laid the sick in the streets, and besought him that they might touch if it were but the border of his garment: and as many as touched him were made whole."—Mark 6:54–56.

The disciples and Jesus went right back to work the next day. I challenge you to show me anyplace in this account where they actually got to rest. Not only did they not get the day of rest that they had planned, they missed a night's sleep. Then as soon as they got to shore, the cycle of ministry started up again.

In the passage most often cited as an excuse to quit responsibility in order to have rest, the disciples didn't get any rest. I've heard 'come apart and rest' used to justify quitting a bus route. I've had people quote it to me when they were telling me they were going to quit teaching their Sunday school classes.

If people actually read the Bible, they'd find out it doesn't say what they've been told it says. Stopping to rest was the original plan, but it didn't work out that way. The needs of the people were

5

more important to Jesus than His own need for rest.

The apostle Paul never burned out.

"Are they ministers of Christ? (I speak as a fool) I am more; in labours more abundant, in stripes above measure, in prisons more frequent, in deaths oft.

"Of the Jews five times received I forty stripes save one.

"Thrice was I beaten with rods, once was I stoned, thrice I suffered shipwreck, a night and a day I have been in the deep;

"In journeyings often, in perils of waters, in perils of robbers, in perils by mine own countrymen, in perils by the heathen, in perils in the city, in perils in the wilderness, in perils in the sea, in perils among false brethren;

"In weariness and painfulness, in watchings often, in hunger and thirst, in fastings often, in cold and nakedness.

"Beside those things that are without, that which cometh upon me daily, the care of all the churches."—II Cor. 11:23–28.

Despite the incredible stress and labor Paul put into the ministry, he never burned out. He survived stoning—the method of execution. He survived shipwreck. He spent an entire twenty-four hours floating in the ocean. He was constantly at work and constantly in danger. Yet he served faithfully to the end of his life. His incredible heavy work load did not make him burn out.

THE CONSEQUENCES TAUGHT

God made us to work for Him.

Ephesians 2:10 says, "For we are his workmanship, created in Christ Jesus unto good works, which God hath before ordained that we should walk in them." You were made to work. That is the purpose of the masterpiece God wrought in creating you—to do good works. Everybody is going to get tired. Somebody once said to me, "By the end of the day, I'm tired." I said, "Go to bed. That's why they made beds." You're supposed to be tired at the end of the day. God made you to work.

Most of our stress problems are really sin problems.

"Be careful for nothing; but in every thing by prayer and suppli-

cation with thanksgiving let your requests be made known unto God.

"And the peace of God, which passeth all understanding, shall keep your hearts and minds through Christ Jesus."—Phil. 4:6, 7.

If we'd replace griping and worrying with praying and praising, we'd have peace instead of stress. Just as the disciples did when Jesus instructed them to feed the multitude, we tend to focus on our shortcomings instead of relying on God. It takes a lot of energy to worry. It takes a lot of energy to complain. It takes a lot of energy to be upset.

God has commanded us to come to Him in prayer rather than allowing our lives to be filled with worry. There is no problem that you face that is too large or too difficult for God. Turn it over to Him, and you will find your strength and energy renewed.

God gives us grace to serve Him.

Grace is supernatural enablement to serve God. Paul had a thorn in his flesh. He asked God three times to remove it. God said no. Second Corinthians 12:9 says, "And he said unto me, My grace is sufficient for thee: for my strength is made perfect in weakness. Most gladly therefore will I rather glory in my infirmities, that the power of Christ may rest upon me."

God's grace is sufficient—it is everything you could possibly need. You may feel like you just don't have energy to do your work. It's important to realize that is wasn't going to get done in your energy anyway. Without God's power, you cannot do God's work.

We should take care of our bodies.

Since your body is the temple of the Holy Spirit (I Cor. 6:19), it deserves proper care and attention. In addition, your body is the physical instrument you use to serve God. The great Scottish preacher, Robert Murray McCheyne, was mightily used by God to spread revival across Scotland. His journal had a great impact on the life of the missionary David Brainerd.

Yet McCheyne was so eager to work that he completely neglected to care for his health. He died before he was thirty years old. On his deathbed he told a friend, "God gave me a message to deliver and a horse to ride. I have killed the horse and can no longer deliver the message."

I believe you should exercise. Get the sleep that you need. Take

7

care of your body. I eat better now than I once did. I go to the salad bar at the restaurant. I even eat broccoli on purpose sometimes. Take care of your body so that you can continue to work for God.

We should take better care of our soul and spirit than we do of our bodies.

First Timothy 4:8 says, "For bodily exercise profiteth little: but godliness is profitable unto all things, having promise of the life that now is, and of that which is to come." What's on the inside in your spirit affects what's on the outside—your body. Sin harbored in the heart harms the body (Ps. 32:1–4).

Rather than focusing primarily on the body, we need to ensure that our spirit is right with God. Pray with thanksgiving. Think on things that are good, pure, lovely, honest and just. The things on which you meditate determine your outlook on life.

Burnout is not caused by working the flesh too hard; it is caused by working too hard *in* the flesh.

There are frankly very few people who work themselves into an early grave. Such people would be like Mark Twain's well-behaved church choir. He said there was one once, but it was so long ago that no one seems to be able to say exactly where it was! My biggest problem over the years has not been any great need to slow people down.

You don't burn a motor out early by running it; you burn it out early by running it without oil. Running in the flesh without the Holy Spirit's power wears on a Christian. We have the resources of God at our disposal. If we depend on His strength, ingenuity and resources rather than our own, we will not burn out, no matter how difficult the challenges we may face.

"Hast thou not known? hast thou not heard, that the everlasting God, the LORD, the Creator of the ends of the earth, fainteth not, neither is weary? there is no searching of his understanding.

"He giveth power to the faint; and to them that have no might he increaseth strength.

"Even the youths shall faint and be weary, and the young men shall utterly fall:

"But they that wait upon the LORD shall renew their strength; they shall mount up with wings as eagles; they shall run, and not be weary; and they shall walk, and not faint."—Isa. 40:28–31.

CHAPTER TWO
WERE THE MEN IN ACTS 6 ACTUALLY DEACONS?

If you asked most Christians, they would tell you that the first deacons were the men selected in Acts, chapter 6, to take care of the needs of the widows in the church at Jerusalem. This idea is so often referenced that most people accept it without ever stopping to think about what the Scripture actually says.

There are many good people who believe this. Much greater Christians who have done more for the work of the Lord than I ever will hold this belief. Dr. John R. Rice, in the Rice Reference Bible, has this footnote for Acts 6: "These seven men, we suppose, were the first deacons. Note first that they were servants of the church. 'Deacon' is the Anglicized Greek word for 'servant.' These men were to care for poor widows in the church."

In addition to looking in depth at whether the men in Acts 6 were deacons, we will also examine the impact that belief has on church government in our day.

THE COMMON TEACHING

It is the common teaching that the seven men named in Acts 6—Stephen, Philip, Prochorus, Nicanor, Timon, Parmenas and Nicolas—were the first deacons. Their service sets a pattern for the duties and responsibilities of deacons today. Here's how the teaching is normally set forth.

The Greek word *diakonos* is used to describe these men.

Although the word "deacon" does not appear in Acts, chapter 6, in the King James Bible, that is the underlying Greek word that

9

describes the work these men were to do. As noted by Dr. Rice in his comments on this passage, *deacon* is simply the Anglicized form of the Greek word that we use today to describe this office within the church.

I was taught a very important lesson by a professor name Dick Rupp when I was in college. He was one of the best teachers I ever had. He said, "Before you go to commentaries, read the Bible. After you get everything you can out of the Bible, then go to the commentaries." Dr. Rupp also described the process by which errors can be transmitted.

Suppose someone writes a good commentary but gets one item wrong. Because the overall commentary is good, it becomes widely used. In the next generation, the people who write commentaries pick up and repeat the error because it is in a widely used commentary. Thus, wrong interpretations of Scripture get passed down from one generation to the next.

Don't ever be afraid to use just the Bible. God didn't inspire the commentaries. I'm all for commentaries, and I believe in study. I have a library full of tools that I use to prepare sermons and lessons, but they are not the final authority. The Word of God is.

The deacons were chosen to handle the business matters of the church.

Many churches have a number of committees. Frequently those committees assume an unhealthy authority in the church. There are many churches where this happens, but I recall well one particular case where the pastor tried to hide behind the deacons. He had the board of deacons issue any policies that he thought would be unpopular or controversial.

One of the issues that came up in that church was whether to remarry people who had been previously divorced. So the deacons met and talked about it at some length. Finally they issued a policy that said, "The pastor is directed not to perform weddings where one of the parties has been divorced." I remember that when I heard that I wondered why he was not willing just to come out and say what he believed.

In fact, he later said, "It's harder for people to get mad at eight men than it is for them to get mad at me." That's how many pastors use the deacons. They become the authority in the church for situations that the pastor doesn't want to address. In my experience, when deacons or committees take over that kind of responsibility, the pastor will have a very difficult time exercising effective leadership in the church.

The disciples focused on spiritual matters.

It is true that the disciples said to the church, "We will give ourselves continually to prayer, and to the ministry of the word" (Acts 6:4). However, this was not an abdication by the disciples of responsibility or interest in the management of the church. They simply could not physically accomplish everything that needed to be done. So the church selected men to handle one particular responsibility, thus relieving the apostles of the need to take food to the widows in the church.

Deacons are to handle the financial affairs of the church, and the pastor is to care for spiritual concerns.

This is the conclusion of the common teaching. Those who hold this belief draw a line of division between the "business" and "spiritual" aspects of church leadership. However, even if the men in Acts 6 were deacons, that would still not serve as a pattern for such a decision of responsibility within the church.

The only task those seven men had was to take food to the widows each day. They were appointed to that task by the disciples. There is nothing in Scripture to suggest that these men had any responsibility or authority at all in any other church business.

You may have heard the old joke about the couple who had been married thirty years and told people that they had never had a single fight. Someone asked them what their secret was. The husband replied, "We agreed when we got married that I would make the big decisions and she would make the small decisions. In thirty years of marriage, we've never had a big decision, so there's never been anything to fight about!"

It's like that in a lot of churches that hold this common teaching. The line between spiritual matters and business matters gets blurred, and the deacons come to assume more and more responsibility. There are many churches where the pastor has very little authority at all.

Years ago the deacon chairman of a church other than mine

11

came by to see me. His church was looking for a pastor, and he asked if I thought my dad would be interested in the job. I told him, "He might; but if my dad comes, he will be the pastor."

He said, "Yes, we believe that. We want the pastor to lead the church. Of course the deacons are going to watch him and make sure he doesn't do anything wrong."

Now accountability is a good thing, but there is nothing in the Bible that says the deacons are to watch the pastor and govern his ministry. There is a church not too far from where I pastor where the church constitution specifically says the deacons are the spiritual leaders of the church. I sometimes wonder what the pastor does in that church.

We had a man in our church who didn't like something I had announced I was going to preach. He went to the deacons and asked them if they thought it was right for me to preach on that topic. They told him, "We don't make those decisions. Talk to the pastor." There is no Bible model for deacons' dictating or ruling either business or spiritual decisions.

THE CONTRADICTORY TRUTH

There are several problems with believing that Acts 6 is a description of the first deacons.

The men in Acts 6 are never called deacons.

At no point in the scriptural account is the position these seven men held called an office. The Greek word *diakonos* is used three times. In verse 1, it is translated "ministration." In verse 2, it is translated "serve." It is used in verse 4 in the phrase "the ministry of the word." The word simply means "to serve," and it is used throughout the Bible to describe a servant.

The use of this same word in verse 4 is critical to understanding the passage. It describes, not the work of the seven men serving food to the widows, but the work of the apostles in preaching and teaching the Bible.

Clearly then we cannot conclude just from the Greek word used that the seven men chosen in Acts 6 were deacons. That would require us to believe that the apostles were also deacons, since the same descriptive word is used of them.

12

The requirements for deacons in I Timothy 3 are entirely different from the requirements in Acts 6.

There is not a single overlapping qualification on the two lists. Acts 6:3 says that the men chosen must be "of honest report, full of the Holy Ghost and wisdom." But the list in I Timothy is very different.

"Likewise must the deacons be grave, not doubletongued, not given to much wine, not greedy of filthy lucre;

"Holding the mystery of the faith in a pure conscience.

"And let these also first be proved; then let them use the office of a deacon, being found blameless.

"Even so must their wives be grave, not slanderers, sober, faithful in all things.

"Let the deacons be the husbands of one wife, ruling their children and their own houses well."—I Tim. 3:8–12.

The Bible is clear that the deacons are to be proven, tested, honorable men. Certainly the men in Acts 6 were outstanding men; but since their requirements were so different from those given in I Timothy 3, it is certainly reasonable to question whether they were actually deacons. They are never called deacons, nor is any reference made to the idea of their having an office.

The Bible word *diakonos* is used many times in Scripture where it could not be referring to deacons.

Luke 10:40 says, "Martha was cumbered about much serving"; but not very many people would argue that the use of the word *diakonos* to describe her makes her a deacon. Luke 17:8 uses the same word when it says, "Make ready wherewith I may sup, and gird thyself, and serve me." The house servant putting the meal on the table was certainly not a deacon in the church.

In John 12:26 Jesus said, "If any man serve me, let him follow me." Again this word clearly is not being used to describe deacons. To say the men in Acts 6 were deacons because they were appointed to serve ignores the repeated uses of that same word in other places in the Bible where it is used of people who were not deacons.

The pastor, not the deacons, is to take care of the church.

If you look at the qualifications for church offices given in

13

I Timothy 3, you will find many parallels between the pastor and the deacons. Each is required to be blameless, the husband of one wife, ruling his house well, not having a problem with alcohol and not being motivated by greed.

But look at what is said about the pastor in verse 5: "For if a man know not how to rule his own house, how shall he take care of the church of God?" Scripture does not say that about the deacons in this passage or anywhere else. In fact, there is no place in the Word of God that gives the deacons *any* leadership role in the church. The title of their office is a word that means "servant."

God places the responsibility of leadership, the "care of the church of God," on the shoulders of the pastor. The same Greek word is used in Luke 10:35 when the Good Samaritan told the innkeeper, "Take care of him." According to *Vine's Expository Dictionary*, the word indicates foresight, provision and focusing on the needs of others.

Simply put, God holds the pastor accountable for both the spiritual and business well-being of the church and its members (Heb. 13:17). Since he will answer to God, he needs to take responsibility for the decisions that are made and the direction the church takes.

There is no place in the Bible where a deacon ever makes a decision for a church.

We have wonderful deacons at our church. They are good men with good hearts who care about the church. We get along wonderfully. I am thankful to God for giving us such dedicated men. However, their significance as deacons lies in their service, not in their leadership. That is the pattern established in Scripture.

I count on the advice and input of these godly men; I look for their help; but since God holds me ultimately responsible for the First Baptist Church of Bridgeport, I pastor the church. I am the leader, not because I desire power, but because that is the way God intended for the church to function.

Years ago I asked our deacons to study the Bible and find out what the duties of deacons are. They came back and said they couldn't find any. That was not because they were poor Bible students; it was because there is no place in Scripture that gives the deacons any specific responsibility to make decisions or lead the church.

THE CONSEQUENCES TAUGHT

Looking at the history and proper role of deacons leads us to these conclusions.

Tradition does not equal truth.

It's very easy to fall into the habit of doing something because "we've always done it that way." There are some traditions that are good and helpful. When there are effective ways to do things, it's fine to stick with them; but just because something is a tradition doesn't mean it is true.

We traditionally have a candlelight service around Christmastime at our church; but if we didn't have it one year, we would not be disobeying the Bible. When I came to First Baptist Church of Bridgeport, they elected all kinds of officers. They elected the Sunday school superintendent, the treasurer and the church clerk.

The Bible teaches there are only two offices in the church, so we quit having those elections. They had been doing things that way for a long time, but there was no Bible basis for the practice. Our goal is to try to do things as close to the pattern in the Word of God as we can.

The problem with tradition is that we can easily accept as right things that are contrary to God's plan. Jesus said,

"But ye say, Whosoever shall say to his father or his mother, It is a gift, by whatsoever thou mightest be profited by me;

"And honour not his father or his mother, he shall be free. Thus have ye made the commandment of God of none effect by your tradition."—Matt. 15:5, 6.

Practice is not always based on principle.

Maybe you have heard the story about a certain young couple who got married. The first time his new wife fixed a pot roast, the husband watched in amazement as she sliced off both ends before putting it into the pot. "How come you're cutting off the ends?" he asked. "My mother always did it that way," she replied.

15

After some discussion, they called her mother and asked why she cut off the ends of the roast before cooking it. "When we first got married," she said, " I had a pot that was too little to put a whole pot roast in. So I'd trim off both ends to make it fit"!

When I was a student in college, the girl students were allowed to iron clothes in their dorm rooms, but the boys were not. Someone asked why the rule was different for girls and boys. The first person he asked didn't know why the rule was there. After some investigation, he found that the electrical current in some of the old buildings had not been sufficient for all the appliances.

Though the problem with the electricity had been corrected years earlier, the rule was still in place. There was no principle involved in the rule, so there was no problem in getting it changed once it was properly brought to the attention of the right people.

Widespread unscriptural practices can occur when we accept as gospel things that aren't so.

A preacher who was a friend of mine left a church he had started and went to pastor another church a few years ago. The new church had about sixty people when he got there. He was faithful to preach and emphasize soul winning, and the church began to grow.

One day he was sitting in his office when one of the deacons came in. The deacon said, "You may be the pastor of this church, but I'm the manager." The pastor had his Bible on his desk. He picked it up and said, "That's interesting. I've read this several times, and I've never found that. Would you show it to me, please." Of course the deacon couldn't show it to him, but he still thought he should be the manager of the church.

That deacon is hardly alone in his belief—but he is wrong. The Bible teaches that the pastor is to be the leader of the church. All sorts of problems arise when we substitute tradition for what Scripture says. We have generations of Christians who have bought into the false concept that the deacons are responsible for the business of the church rather than the pastor.

This has had a negative impact on good churches, as it has diminished the role and authority of the pastor. If we would go back to the Bible rather than tradition to determine our practice, we would be spared these negative effects. One of the purposes of this chapter is to encourage you to study God's Word rather than relying on what you have always been told. In every church we need a revival of commitment to doing things God's way.

CHAPTER THREE
IS A WIFE ALWAYS RESPONSIBLE TO OBEY HER HUSBAND?

Of all the commonly believed teachings that we are examining, perhaps this one has had the greatest impact on the largest number of people. This concept of submission as total obedience by a wife to her husband, without any exceptions, is widely preached and taught. There was a time in my own life when I believed it; but after further study and waiting upon the Lord to show me what the Bible actually does say regarding this matter, I have changed my mind.

I will never forget counseling with a lady whose sincere but misguided belief in absolute submission to her husband caused her untold misery. This sincere, sweet, faithful Christian wife had a backslidden husband. Not content to ruin his own life only and no doubt under conviction from his wife's testimony "without the word," he pressured her to join him in his wicked behavior.

At first, he required her to go with him when he went to the bar. Later, he began insisting that she join him in drinking alcoholic beverages. Ultimately, he demanded her complete degradation by ordering her to engage in an immoral affair with one of his "friends."

She looked at me with tears in her eyes and said, "I was taught I should always obey my husband." Her life was in ruins, not just because of her husband's wicked behavior, but because she had not been properly taught the limits of obedience to his authority.

Yet even in the face of tragedies like that, many people continue to teach that a wife must always obey her husband, without any exceptions.

THE COMMON TEACHING

Here are the foundations of this teaching:

A wife is always to obey her husband.

Like most of the concepts we've examined herein, there is an element of truth that has expanded to become something the Bible does not support. The Word of God clearly does teach that God has ordained for the husband to be the head of the home and for the wife to be in submission to him.

From this doctrine, the proponents of this common teaching declare that a wife is always to obey her husband without exception. They note that God does not tell a wife to be in submission to her husband unless he's unreasonable. Arguing from the standpoint of the silence of Scripture on this point of making an exception to the wife's submission to her husband, they say that this proves there are no such exceptions.

If the husband requires his wife to do wrong, God will not hold her responsible.

This teaching relies on the concept that there is an umbrella of protection over everyone. Those who hold this view say that if the authority in your life orders you to do wrong, he will answer to God for it instead of you.

There are situations in which the concept of a protective umbrella of authority is true. For instance, if a lady has no income and her husband refuses to tithe on the money he earns, God will not hold her accountable for it. We do have a responsibility to obey whatever authority God places over us (Rom. 13:1–6). The error of this common teaching is that it fails to recognize that there are other commandments which must be obeyed as well.

Dr. Bob Jones, Sr., used to say, "Duties never conflict." His point was not that there would never be competing claims on our time or choices that would have to be made. Rather, he was saying that there is always an overriding, most important duty that will guide our behavior when we must choose between two responsibilities.

A wife cannot use obedience to God as an excuse to disobey her husband.

Those who promote this teaching say that since God commanded obedience to her husband, a wife cannot appeal to His law when her husband wants her to do something. The most common objection to this teaching is, "But what if the husband orders his wife to do something that would force her to disobey God?" The answer is usually something along the lines of, "God is the one who told her she should always obey her husband in the first place."

I have already shared with you the sad story of the woman who was directed into immorality by her husband. No matter where you come down philosophically on the question of a wife's duty to obey, when you get to the sometimes tragic consequences of this teaching, they have to make you cringe.

Usually when they're faced with a serious situation like this, the proponents of this teaching will say, "If the wife had done all she could have to be the right kind of wife, her husband would never have required that of her." That's blaming the victim. Sin on one person's part is never an excuse for another person to sin.

THE CONTRADICTORY TRUTH

God's command for Christians to obey government is at least as clear and forceful as His command for wives to obey their husbands.

"Let every soul be subject unto the higher powers. For there is no power but of God: the powers that be are ordained of God.

"Whosoever therefore resisteth the power, resisteth the ordinance of God: and they that resist shall receive to themselves damnation.

"For rulers are not a terror to good works, but to the evil. Wilt thou then not be afraid of the power? do that which is good, and thou shalt have praise of the same:

"For he is the minister of God to thee for good. But if thou do that which is evil, be afraid; for he beareth not the sword in vain: for he is the minister of God, a revenger to execute wrath upon him that doeth evil.

"Wherefore ye must needs be subject, not only for wrath, but also for conscience sake."—Rom. 13:1–5.

"Wives, submit yourselves unto your own husbands, as unto the Lord.

"For the husband is the head of the wife, even as Christ is the

head of the church: and he is the saviour of the body.

"Therefore as the church is subject unto Christ, so let the wives be to their own husbands in every thing."—Eph. 5:22–24.

It's interesting to me that Ephesians 5 does not spell out the same kind of consequences for disobedience to husbands that Romans 13 spells out for disobedience to government. We have an obligation to obey civil authorities. We need to be good citizens and maintain a good testimony. That's why Jesus paid taxes even though He wasn't obligated to do so (Matt. 17:24–27).

Think about the government that was in place when Paul wrote Romans 13. Nero, the emperor of Rome, was one of the most corrupt rulers in history. He burned Christians on poles to light his gardens at night for his parties. Yet Paul commanded by inspiration that the Roman believers were to obey the authority of Nero, because he was "ordained of God."

God notes and commends those who disobey government in order to obey Him.

The command to obey government is not an absolute commandment. The same apostle Paul who was inspired by the Holy Spirit to write, "Let every soul be subject unto the higher powers" was a jailbird. He went to jail for willfully disobeying the government. He continued preaching when he had been told to stop.

So we see that there are some circumstances when we should *not* obey authority. However, while obedience is not an absolute, submission is an absolute. You must either obey the law or submit to the penalty. Paul disobeyed the law and suffered the penalty for continuing to preach, yet he never struck back against his guards. Paul just used the opportunity to witness to the guards who were chained to him. He started a church in jail. He did not obey, but neither did he resist the government.

In Exodus 1 there is an amazing story. Pharaoh commanded the Hebrew midwives to kill any boy babies that were born. He was worried about the growing numbers of Hebrews in his kingdom; and he thought that by killing off the boys, he could effect a means of population control.

Because the midwives feared God (Exod. 1:17), they refused to obey the pharaoh's wicked order. When they were called to account for their disobedience, they lied about what they had done. I think it would have been better for them to have told the truth, but there is no question concerning what God thought about their refusal to obey Pharaoh.

"Therefore God dealt well with the midwives: and the people multiplied, and waxed very mighty.

"And it came to pass, because the midwives feared God, that he made them houses."—Exod. 1:20,21.

God rewarded the midwives for their disobedience to the government by giving them families of their own. That is the meaning of the Hebrew idiom translated into English as "made them houses."

In Acts, chapter 5, we see the story of the council forbidding the apostles to preach in Jesus' name. Although the Roman governor was the ultimate authority, in an effort to keep the peace, he had delegated to the Jewish religious leaders the power to govern religious matters.

Acts 5:29 says, "Then Peter and the other apostles answered and said, We ought to obey God rather than men." That is still true today. If the choice actually is between obeying God and obeying man, there is no question about what we should do.

Be careful to make sure that you are actually obeying God before you make the decision to disobey authority. A few years ago there was a pastor who led his church to rebel against the government's authority. He decided that they did not need to have anything to do with the government. He refused to pay employment taxes for church employees. He encouraged people not to be involved with the government. Tragically, what was once a large church that saw many people saved was sold off to pay a tax bill they should have never owed.

Don't go your own way and justify it by saying you are obeying God.

The Bible teaches that church members are supposed to follow and obey their pastors (Heb. 13:17). Suppose your pastor got up on Wednesday night and said, "I want everyone to pick out a convenience store on the way home tonight and rob it so we can have a good offering on Sunday." It would be foolish to obey him if he told you to do something like that which contradicts the Word of God.

23

In the same way, it is wrong for a wife to disobey God for the sake of obeying her husband. If his decisions are truly contrary to God's will as revealed in His Word, a wife should not obey him. It is never right to do wrong just because someone in authority tells you to do so.

God gives us an example of a wife who acted contrary to her husband's wishes and was commended.

When David was fleeing for his life from King Saul, he came in contact with a man named Nabal. The Bible says he was "churlish and evil in his doings" (I Sam. 25:3). Despite the fact that David's followers had not taken any of his sheep, as was the common practice of soldiers in that day, and had even protected his workers (I Sam. 25:16), Nabal refused David's request for help.

Word of that came back to David, and he prepared his men to go to battle against Nabal. Nabal and his sheepherders would have had no chance of survival against David's men of war. When word reached Abigail, Nabal's wife, of her husband's foolish decision, she took matters into her own hands.

Without telling her husband, she ordered food to be prepared for David and his men. She personally went and begged for David's forgiveness for her husband's rash behavior. That was not what her husband wanted, but his pride and folly were about to get everyone in his house killed. In response to her plea for mercy, David agreed to spare Nabal. God killed Abigail's husband, and she married David. She did the right thing in acting contrary to her husband's ungodly decision.

The story of Achan demonstrates that those under authority are not exempt from punishment for disobedience.

"So Joshua sent messengers, and they ran unto the tent; and, behold, it was hid in his tent, and the silver under it.

"And they took them out of the midst of the tent, and brought them unto Joshua, and unto all the children of Israel, and laid them out before the LORD.

"And Joshua, and all Israel with him, took Achan the son of Zerah, and the silver, and the garment, and the wedge of gold, and

his sons, and his daughters, and his oxen, and his asses, and his sheep, and his tent, and all that he had: and they brought them unto the valley of Achor.

"And Joshua said, Why hast thou troubled us? the LORD shall trouble thee this day. And all Israel stoned him with stones, and burned them with fire, after they had stoned them with stones."— Josh. 7:22–25.

Why did Achan's wife have to die? She did not steal anything. Why did his children have to die? The answer is found in the location of the stolen goods. They were under the floor of his tent. Achan's wife and children were accessories after the fact to his theft.

Even though they didn't steal anything from the city of Jericho, they went along with what Achan did. I believe they knew that Achan had done wrong and they didn't do anything about it. That garment from Babylon may have looked pretty good to Achan's wife. The gold and silver would have set the kids up with all the latest toys. They were held responsible and stoned to death, even though they were under the "umbrella of authority" Achan held in the home as the husband and father.

THE CONSEQUENCES TAUGHT

All human authority is limited by God's authority.

No authority, whether government official, pastor or husband, has the right to tell anyone under him to do something that disobeys God. Human authority is never absolute. God's Word has set boundaries that we are always to follow.

Different people draw lines in different places. Our church supports missionaries in China who are completely "underground." They attempt to keep everything they do out of sight because the government would persecute them if their actions were found out. We support another missionary who, because of his relationship with the Philippine government, was able to get permission from the Chinese government to start churches. He has started more than thirty open churches in mainland China.

At the dedication of one of those new church buildings, a Communist Party official came and spoke. He said, "It is okay to love your religion. Be sure you love your government too." I've been invited to go and speak in one of those churches allowed by the government, and I'm looking forward to getting that opportunity.

There may come a day when such missionaries will not be able to continue to operate like they do now. If that happens, I believe they will stand up for what is right and say, "No, we won't compromise what we believe to get your approval." They are working with the government, but if they were forced to choose, they would obey God rather than men.

A wife should seek alternatives that will allow her to please both God and her husband.

I have known of a husband's trying to force his wife into something that was clearly disobedient to God, partly because she would not cooperate in other areas that did not involve obedience to God. That did not justify the husband in his expecting his wife to do something wrong. However, a wife is responsible to try to please her husband in every possible way that does not violate the Word of God.

I know some ladies who won't cook meals the way their husbands like them. They think their way is better. A wise husband will not make a habit of focusing on minor issues. He won't try to force everything to be his way; but if he has a color preference, his wife should wear that color frequently. If he likes his food a certain way, she should cook it that way.

A wife who submits in all possible areas without doing wrong will usually not be asked to submit in a way that would force her to disobey God.

It is not right to say that a wife who is submissive will never be asked to do wrong. However, that usually is the case. If a wife is working to please and honor her husband, that will have a powerful impact on his attitude and behavior toward her.

A wife must never disobey God in order to obey her husband.

A Christian should never disobey God, no matter what the situation is. There are times when you may have to suffer for the sake of righteousness.

There's a great example of this in the story of Daniel. He was a teenage boy when he was carried away captive to Babylon. The training program of the Babylonians offered him food from the king's table.

Daniel had already made up his mind not to defile himself in the heathen land (Dan. 1:8). He requested permission from the immediate authority over him to try a different approach. His alternative was a diet that would allow him to obey the law of God. At the end of the ten days, Daniel and his friends looked better than those who ate the king's food (Dan. 1:15). In that case, they did not have to disobey the king in order to obey God.

However, when Daniel's enemies tricked the king into signing a decree stating that no one could pray to any god except the king for thirty days, there was no way to appeal. So, despite the law that had been passed, Daniel obeyed God. He went to his room as he always did and knelt in prayer (Dan. 6:10).

Because Daniel obeyed God, he ended up being thrown into the den of lions. He was willing to suffer for righteousness rather than do wrong.

There is never a circumstance when disobeying God is justified. It is wrong for Christians to teach women that they are to obey their husbands even if they are told to do something wicked. This teaching, though common, is contrary to the clear and repeated emphasis of Scripture.

CHAPTER FOUR
WILL GOD POUR OUT UNBELIEVABLE BLESSINGS IF WE TITHE?

There seems to be something about money that affects people more than almost anything else. Thefts, murders, embezzling, immorality, drug sales—things that would horrify most people in the abstract are all committed in pursuit of money. When asked how much it would take to satisfy him, both John D. Rockefeller and J. Paul Getty is each reported to have said, "A few dollars more." Which of them said it first is inconsequential; the sad truth is, their answer aptly describes the heart of man.

In addition to leading people to do strange and sometimes evil things in an attempt to get money, the desire for wealth also leads some to change their doctrinal teaching. A great example of this is found in a common teaching about giving. Based on an interpretation of Malachi 3:10, some say that God will pour out unbelievable blessings on those who tithe.

THE COMMON TEACHING

It is commonly taught that God will bless those who tithe beyond their ability to receive.

Malachi 3:10 says, "Bring ye all the tithes into the storehouse, that there may be meat in mine house, and prove me now herewith, saith the LORD of hosts, if I will not open you the windows of heaven, and pour you out a blessing, that there shall not be room enough to receive it."

At first glance, this teaching appears to be exactly what Malachi 3:10 says. However, we will see that this teaching does not stand up to careful investigation.

29

Not long ago, I asked our church members, "How many of you have ever had to go to God and say, 'Lord, I can't take any more blessing. I've got money in every bank in town that exceeds the FDIC insurance. Lord, please, no more. I've had more blessings than I can receive'?" Not a single person said yes.

If you've never said that, does that mean you don't tithe? Clearly there must be a problem with the common interpretation of this verse. If you tithe and you haven't received that level of blessing, is the Bible wrong in what it says? Of course not. If the Bible says one thing and your experience says another, you must always believe the Bible. Experience is faulty.

Mark Twain told a story about his cat jumping on the wood stove during the winter and getting burned. He said the cat never jumped on the stove again even in the middle of summer. The cat thought that what happened one time was guaranteed in the future. Experience, however, is not a suitable foundation for doctrine.

The problem is *never* with the Bible. If there are things we don't understand, we should simply be reminded that the Bible is above our understanding. It is God's Book. It was written for man, but there are things in it that we're not always able to understand. We need to base our doctrine and practice on the Word of God, properly interpreted and applied.

The word "window" in Malachi refers, not to an actual window, but to special wisdom or insight.

Another facet of the common teaching is that tithing opens a window. The proponents of this doctrine say that you don't get things through windows; you get things through doors. So, they say, when God talks about opening a window, He is talking about giving you the ability to have special insight and wisdom.

The proponents of this teaching say that when you tithe, you see how to be a better parent, a better worker, a better spouse. They take Malachi 3:10 to be metaphorical rather than to mean that God will actually give you material blessing as a reward for tithing.

Each individual who tithes will be amazingly blessed.

The bottom line of the teaching is that, whether financial or spiritual, the promise of God is that He will give amazing blessings to those who tithe.

30

THE CONTRADICTORY TRUTH

God *does* command tithing.

Leviticus 27:30 says, "And all the tithe of the land, whether of the seed of the land, or of the fruit of the tree, is the LORD'S: it is holy unto the LORD." The tithe belongs to God. If you keep it, you are stealing from God. It is holy unto God, meaning that it is sanctified, or set apart. It belongs especially to Him.

Some people object to tithing on the basis that it is an Old Testament doctrine; but in the New Testament, Jesus said to the Pharisees, "Woe unto you, scribes and Pharisees, hypocrites! for ye pay tithe of mint and anise and cumin, and have omitted the weightier matters of the law, judgment, mercy, and faith: these ought ye to have done, and not to leave the other undone" (Matt. 23:23).

Jesus did not condemn the Pharisees for tithing; He commended them for tithing. You'll search long and hard to find good things Jesus said about the Pharisees. Yet in this one instance, Jesus praised their behavior because they were careful to tithe even on the herbs that they grew.

Four hundred years before the Law was given to Moses, Abraham paid tithes to Melchizedek (Gen. 14:17–20). Tithing is an eternal principle. It was practiced before the Law. Jacob promised to tithe when he saw his vision of the angels of God at Bethel (Gen. 28:10–22). When God gave Moses the Law, tithing was an integral part of it (Lev. 27:30; Num. 18:24–26; Deut. 12:6).

So tithing was practiced before the Law, commanded under the Law, and commended by Jesus who came to fulfill the Law.

Part of the reason people object to tithing is that they do not understand the reason God commands it. God certainly does not need our money. The point of tithing is to establish in our minds God's ownership of everything and to help us learn to fear Him properly.

"Thou shalt truly tithe all the increase of thy seed, that the field bringeth forth year by year.

"And thou shalt eat before the LORD thy God, in the place which he shall choose to place his name there, the tithe of thy corn, of thy wine, and of thine oil, and the firstlings of thy herds and of thy

flocks; that thou mayest learn to fear the LORD thy God always."— Deut. 14:22, 23.

God calls those who don't tithe thieves.

Suppose someone got up at offering time in your church and prayed, "Dear Heavenly Father, thank You for giving us the opportunity to give back a portion of what You have given us. I pray that You would bless those who obey and judge the crooks." That wouldn't be politically correct, but it would be scripturally correct.

Malachi 3:8 says, "Will a man rob God? Yet ye have robbed me. But ye say, Wherein have we robbed thee? In tithes and offerings." The Bible makes it very clear that those who do not tithe rob God.

Dr. Paul Chappell told me about a special night they had at their church a while back. They had about 150 bus kids in the auditorium on a Sunday night for the evening service. There was one boy they had to stop from taking money out of the offering plate as it came by. He just didn't quite get the concept of an offering!

If you were low on gas and knew you weren't going to get paid till Friday, would you take a little out when the offering plate came by? Of course not. We have no problem recognizing that doing that would be stealing, but there is no difference in God's eyes between taking money out of the offering plate and failing to put our money in the plate.

The tithe doesn't become the Lord's once it goes into the offering plate—it is the Lord's. Ten percent of your money belongs to God as soon as it comes into your possession. It has always been His money. It is no less stealing to leave it in your pocket than it is to take it out of the offering plate. The only difference is whether you're taking the money God entrusted to someone else or the money He entrusted to you.

It's interesting to me that tithing is one of only a handful of commands with no human enforcement system set up under the law. Most of the commandments God gave His children had a definite enforcement mechanism to provide punishment if they were violated.

Yet when it comes to tithing, God enforces the punishment Himself. He takes the matter of giving very seriously. In fact, He placed a curse on the nation of Israel because they were keeping His tithe for themselves (Mal. 3:9).

God never promises *individuals* will enjoy blessing beyond their ability to receive.

The promise of Malachi 3:10 was made to the nation of Israel. Malachi 3:9 makes the context very clear as God says His curse has been placed on "this whole nation." God is talking to the nation of Israel. It is a violation of good Bible interpretation to say that the promise of verse 10 is addressed to individuals.

There is a *principle* for individuals in this passage, but the promised blessing is for the nation. God said He would pour out a blessing if "ye" bring the tithes. "Ye" is a plural pronoun. It is not used for an individual. If the promise were for individuals, the language would be "Bring thee" or "Bring thou" the tithes. It is an error to apply this passage in a way God didn't intend it to be taken and used.

THE CONSEQUENCES TAUGHT

Bible doctrine must always be taken in context.

I heard about a man who was reading his Bible using the "open and point" method. He prayed that God would direct him to verses that would show him what he should do. The first verse he found said, "[Judas] went and hanged himself." He didn't think that was what God was saying, so he opened his Bible again. The second verse he found said, "Go, and do thou likewise." He thought he'd give it one more try, but the third verse he opened to said, "That thou doest, do quickly."

The Bible is not a spiritual Ouija board. Don't turn the Bible into a fortune-telling device. Read and study the Bible systematically. In II Timothy 2:15, Paul said, "Study to shew thyself approved unto God, a workman that needeth not to be ashamed, rightly dividing the word of truth."

The words translated "rightly dividing" in our English Bible carry the idea of "cutting straight." Have you ever put a hardwood floor in your house? If the wood pieces aren't straight to begin with, it's impossible to get the floor to come out right. In the same way, we need to be careful to use God's Word carefully, letting it mean everything God intended but not reading our preconceptions into it.

Don't use Scripture out of context. A few years ago, there was a pastor not too far from our church who preached an entire sermon from the phrase in Jeremiah 23:28, "The prophet that hath a dream, let him tell a dream." He told his people all about the dreams he had for the church. He told them how he wanted the church to grow and change and move ahead.

It's not bad to have dreams for what you want God to do, but that pastor did not 'rightly divide' God's Word to his people. The next phrase in the same verse says, "...and he that hath my word, let him speak my word faithfully." The whole point God is making in that verse is that a person's dreams don't carry weight like His Word does. In fact, later in the verse, God compares our dreams to chaff and His Word to wheat. That pastor may have delivered a motivational speech, but it was not Bible preaching.

There is an amusing story about an Amish man whose buggy was hit by a car. He sued the driver of the car for $250,000. When the attorney for the driver put the Amish man on the witness stand, he asked, "Isn't it true that right after the accident you told the police officer, 'I've never felt better in my life'?" The Amish man said, "Yes." The lawyer then asked, "Well, then, why are you suing my client?"

The Amish man replied, "Well, you have to take my statement in context. My horse was badly injured in the wreck. When the policeman saw how much the horse was suffering, he pulled out his gun and shot the horse. I had my dog with me in the buggy. He was badly injured too. When the policeman saw how much he was suffering, he shot the dog. Then with that gun still in his hand, he walked up and asked me, 'And how do you feel?' That's when I said, 'I've never felt better in my life!'"

Look at the context when you read and study the Bible. To whom is God speaking? What was He saying to them? What does He say before and after it? How does that apply to your life?

God's Word makes a distinction between tithing and giving.

As we've already seen, the tithe belongs to God (Lev. 27:30, 32). When I tithe, I am discharging an obligation. In all the years we've lived in our home, I've never once received a thank-you note from the mortgage company for making a house payment. Why not? Because I owed those payments to them. They don't owe me thanks for paying a debt.

The tithe is the Lord's. If you let someone borrow your car to run an errand, you don't thank him for giving you a car when he brings

34

it back. It's no big deal to return to someone what already belongs to him. God owes us nothing for giving the tithe back to Him—it belongs to Him.

I pay my taxes to the IRS every year. Do they say thanks? Not exactly. Just try skipping a few years and see what happens. I got a letter audit a few years ago. They wanted me to provide the backup for some deductions I had taken. I sent them what they asked for, and a few weeks later I got a letter that said the item had been decided in my favor, but they did not thank me for paying what I owed.

Supreme Court Justice Oliver Wendell Holmes said, "Taxes are the price we pay for living in a civilized society." I think our taxes are too high. I think a lot of the money we give the government is wasted and some of it goes to things I do not support; but I'd still rather live here than anywhere else on the face of the earth, and paying taxes is our duty as citizens and as Christians.

You *pay* the tithe. You *give* offerings. Offerings are over and above the ten percent we are commanded to give. I believe that you are blessed by God for tithing because it is an act of obedience— just as you are blessed for reading the Bible, being faithful to church, praying, obeying your parents.

However, the greater blessing, the sowing and reaping blessing, is for those who go beyond the tithe and give offerings. God's Word makes a distinction between the two. 'Honoring' God with all that He has given us (Prov. 3:9) produces financial rewards (vs.10).

There is a principle of "multiplication of power."

Leviticus 26:8 says, "And five of you shall chase an hundred, and an hundred of you shall put ten thousand to flight: and your enemies shall fall before you by the sword." This is the same principle that's being taught in Malachi 3. If five chase a hundred, the ratio is 1 to 20. When one hundred put ten thousand to flight, the ratio is 1 to 100. Five people together have power, but one hundred people together have much greater power.

God multiplies blessing when His people join together in His work. In general, if you double the number of people doing the work, you more than double the blessing of God. In some places in the south they have contests called horse pulls to measure the strength of the horses. What they've found is that two horses together can pull an average of twenty times greater weight than one horse can pull alone.

If we could get everyone in a church tithing, the blessings would be multiplied to such an extent that there would be no way to contain them. I asked our financial secretary how much he thought our offerings would increase if everyone who came to our church tithed. His estimate was that giving would nearly double.

You may be familiar with what's called the 80-20 rule. In a normal church, 80% of the money is given by 20% of the people. Typically, the work that is done follows the same pattern. Most of what goes on is done by a minority of the people. If everyone gave, we would have no idea what to do with the money. That's the blessing God is talking about in Malachi 3:10.

There is much that could be done for the work of God. We could completely support missionaries without their having to spend years on deputation to raise the funds to go to the field. We could fund new ministries to reach people for Christ. We could print Bibles and tracts. We could help new churches pay for their buildings so they don't start out with an overwhelming burden of debt.

I have a preacher-friend in Ohio who started a mission church across town from where they met. They bought some property and a small building, but the new church never really took off. After a few years, the area where the building was located experienced a commercial boom. Since the mission church wasn't able to sustain itself, the parent church sold the property for about $200,000 more than they had paid for it.

The church faced a decision about what to do with the money. There were a number of choices they could have made; but they decided that since they had bought the church with missions money, they would use all the proceeds for missions. The pastor took all the missionary letters they had received from the missionaries they supported. They met all the needs for which they had requests from the missionaries.

My pastor-friend said it was one of the most enjoyable times he's ever had in the ministry. The church had more fun meeting those needs than they would have had doing anything for themselves. Wouldn't it be great to be able to do that all the time! That's what would happen if everybody in the church tithed.

When you don't tithe, you're not just robbing God; you're not just leaving God's work without the resources you would have contributed. You're also robbing everyone of the multiplied blessing that could come if everyone would tithe. The windows of Heaven open when God's people together obey His command to tithe. Then we see great resources so that we can do great things for Him.

CHAPTER FIVE

MUST A PASTOR LEAVE THE MINISTRY IF HIS CHILDREN FALL INTO SIN?

Having grown up in the home of a pastor, I have a special affinity for preachers' kids. They face challenges that other children in the church do not face. To a certain extent, they live in a goldfish bowl. At the same time, the pastor faces increased scrutiny over his parenting.

The sad truth is that sometimes preachers' children do fall into sin. Sometimes they abandon what they have learned from their parents and do things they know are wrong. One of the saddest stories I know is that of the famous evangelist Billy Sunday. While he was not a pastor, he was one of the best-known preachers of his day.

He was famous for preaching against the dangers of alcohol. Sunday had himself been a heavy drinker before his salvation. His sermon "Get on the Water Wagon" was one that he preached again and again. Yet his youngest son, Paul, turned to drink and was an alcoholic for much of his life.

Children of preachers do sin. How should the church and the pastor respond when that happens?

THE COMMON TEACHING

Many people believe the Bible teaches that if a pastor's children go into sin, that he should resign from his church and leave the ministry. The common teaching generally follows these points.

The Bible requires a pastor to rule well his own house.

"This is a true saying, If a man desire the office of a bishop, he desireth a good work.

39

"A bishop then must be blameless, the husband of one wife, vigilant, sober, of good behaviour, given to hospitality, apt to teach;

"Not given to wine, no striker, not greedy of filthy lucre; but patient, not a brawler, not covetous;

"One that ruleth well his own house, having his children in subjection with all gravity;

"(For if a man know not how to rule his own house, how shall he take care of the church of God?)"—I Tim. 3:1–5.

There is no question that being a good husband and father is one of the requirements for pastors that Paul gave to Timothy by the inspiration of the Holy Spirit.

The Bible teaches that proper training will produce properly behaved children.

The Bible is filled with commandments and principles for parents to follow in rearing their children. "Train up a child in the way he should go: and when he is old, he will not depart from it" (Prov. 22:6). It would be foolish for us to believe that if we follow the instructions of God's Word, it will not make a difference. If parents do the job God has called them to do in training their children, it will have an impact on the way those children behave, both as children and as adults.

When a child goes wrong, it is always due to a failure on the part of the parents.

Many people believe that if a child doesn't turn out right, the parents must have failed in some way in bringing him up. In the succeeding pages there is a discussion of how this concept ignores one vitally important principle of human behavior. The proponents of the common view hold to the concept that it is always the parents' fault when a child does wrong.

A pastor's child going wrong demonstrates negligence on the part of that pastor.

As a corollary to the previous point, they then conclude that anytime a pastor's child fails, it represents a failure on the part of the parents to train him properly. In this view of things, it is *always* the parents' fault anytime a child goes into sin.

The pastor who rears a wayward child forfeits his right to lead.

The conclusion of this common teaching is that a pastor has forfeited the right to lead a church if his children go astray—that this proves that he is not ruling his own house well as required of pastors by the Word of God.

Make no mistake about it, it is important how you rear your children. I know of one preacher who used to say, "Don't tell me how many you have in Sunday school—let me see your kids." Actually, if I want to evaluate a man, I'm interested in seeing both his church and his family.

I preached not too long ago in Washington for a pastor who has seven children. The oldest is eleven, and most of them are boys! The church is growing and people are being saved. We had sessions from 9:00 to 12:30 Tuesday morning. Those little boys sat there in their black suits and white shirts. If one of them got a little restless, his dad would just look at him, and he'd straighten up. I think that's a wonderful testimony to that pastor. If one of them were to go into sin, would that automatically disqualify their father from pastoring?

THE CONTRADICTORY TRUTH

The Bible *does* require a pastor to rule his house well.

Without any question, a pastor has a definite mandate from God to rear his children properly. Yet in reality, God does not expect less from any other Christian parent. Each of us has a responsibility to "bring them up in the nurture and admonition of the Lord" (Eph. 6:4).

Parents have a great responsibility for their children's behavior.

The behavior of children reflects on their parents. People judge the parents by what they see the children do. Genesis 34 tells the story of Dinah, the daughter of Jacob. She went out to visit some ungodly friends. While she was there, a young man forced himself on her. For some reason he seemed to think that was a good basis for marriage, so he went and asked Jacob for permission to marry her.

41

Jacob's sons were outraged at how their sister was treated. They insisted that the men be circumcised before they would allow the marriage to take place. Then three days later when the men were in pain from the surgery, Simeon and Levi killed all the men of Shechem.

Jacob said, "Ye have troubled me to make me to stink among the inhabitants of the land" (Gen. 34:30). The actions of two of his sons had a definite impact on Jacob's reputation. He knew that he would be held responsible for their deceitful behavior.

Early in I Samuel, we find the story of Eli and Samuel. When Samuel was just a little boy living and working in the tabernacle, God came to him and told him that He was going to judge Eli for not restraining the behavior of his wicked sons. God said, "Behold, I will do a thing in Israel, at which both the ears of every one that heareth it will tingle" (I Sam. 3:11).

God's judgment on Eli and his family is found in I Samuel, chapter 4. Verse 18 says, "And it came to pass, when he made mention of the ark of God, that he fell from off the seat backward by the side of the gate, and his neck brake, and he died: for he was an old man, and heavy. And he had judged Israel forty years."

It's interesting that the Scripture describes Eli as heavy. There weren't very many fat people in Bible times. The lifestyle the people led did not lend itself to gaining weight. There were no all-you-can-eat buffets. The Almond Snicker Bar had not been invented. You really had to be a glutton to get heavy in Bible times.

The priests were allowed to eat part of the sacrifices that the people brought to the tabernacle. They probably ate better than anyone else in Israel prior to the creation of the office of king. I think it's fair to say that Eli indulged his flesh, but he did it in a socially acceptable manner.

Over the years I've heard of a number of preachers having to leave the ministry. Sometimes it was because of immorality. Sometimes it was because of a financial matter. I've never heard of anyone leaving the pulpit because he gained too much weight. I've seen some who did gain a lot, but we don't treat the sin of gluttony quite the same as other sins.

Eli was indulgent of his flesh in one area. His sons were indulgent in many. First Samuel 2:22 says, "Now Eli was very old, and heard all that his sons did unto all Israel; and how they lay with the women that assembled at the door of the tabernacle of the congregation." His sons were immoral. They took the offerings before they were allowed to. Indulging yourself in "acceptable" sins usually leads to your children's indulging themselves in far worse sins. Someone said, "What the parents allow in moderation, the children practice in excess."

The example you set goes far toward determining how your children will behave. The Bible repeatedly says that the sins of the fathers are visited on the children to the third and fourth generations (Exod. 20:5; Num. 14:18; Deut. 5:9). That does not mean that your children pay for your sins. The verses do not say the *penalty* is visited on them; they say the *sins* are visited on them. That means that your children are likely to imitate the sins that you allow in your life.

When he went to the land of Gerar, Abraham lied about his wife because he was afraid that the people would kill him if they knew he was her husband. Sarah was his half-sister, so it wasn't a complete lie; but it was still a lie, intended to deceive. Years later, when a famine arose, Isaac followed his father's footsteps back to Gerar; and out of fear, he lied about his wife. Rebekah was Isaac's cousin several times removed. So, in a sense, Isaac's lie was a bigger lie than the one his father had told.

Then we come to the third generation. Jacob lied about many things. The pattern of sinful behavior was not only repeated from one generation to the next, but it also became worse in the succeeding generations.

There is power from God available to break the chain of family sins. You are not condemned to repeat the mistakes of your parents; but unless you deal with your sins, they will impact your family far into the future.

The Bible also teaches individual soul responsibility.

One of the great doctrines that distinguishes Baptists from people of other beliefs is the concept that everyone answers to God for himself. You don't go through a priest to get to God. You don't get to Heaven by the salvation of your parents.

Romans 14:12 says, "So then every one of us shall give account of himself to God." That means that, no matter what your parents have done, you have no excuse to do wrong. Blaming your parents

43

for your own behavior will have no validity when you stand before God. Our society has adopted a "victim mentality." People think nobody is to blame for anything.

Probably twenty years ago, I turned on the TV in a motel room one afternoon, and Phil Donahue was on. He had as his guest Dr. Stanton Samenow, who is a clinical psychologist. His specialty is working with criminals. He wrote a rather famous book called *Inside the Criminal Mind*. It was fascinating to watch the interview.

Phil Donahue was almost turning purple. He couldn't believe what Dr. Samenow was saying. Dr. Samenow said that people commit crimes because of the way they think. He quoted Proverbs 23:7: "For as he thinketh in his heart, so is he." Donahue didn't want to believe that. He kept talking about people's backgrounds and the disadvantages they experienced as causes for crimes.

Dr. Samenow said, "I'd be glad to believe that; but in my studies I found two children from the same family, who grew up in the same neighborhood, went to the same schools and had the same friends. One is an accountant, and the other is in jail." He said, "You never change the way people behave until you change the way they think." Each of us is responsible before God for what we do or do not do.

God did not remove Eli from leadership because his sons went bad.

First Samuel 3:13 says, "For I have told him that I will judge his house for ever for the iniquity which he knoweth; because his sons made themselves vile, and he restrained them not." God judged Eli, removing him from the office of priest, not because his sons were vile, but because he failed to do anything about it. If Eli had done what was right and his sons had still done wrong, God would have judged only them. Eli was judged for his own sin, not for those of his sons.

It is not the sin of the child that disqualifies a person from leadership. If the leader does not deal with the sin of the child, that disqualifies the leader. A pastor who hides the sin of a child does not meet the biblical qualification of I Timothy 3. I have heard of pastors' taking their teenage daughters to abortion clinics rather than admitting the girls have been immoral. This is perhaps an extreme example of what some pastors will do to try to cover the sins of their children.

THE CONSEQUENCES TAUGHT

There are two balancing truths that must be taken into account.

The Bible teaching on parents and children includes two elements, both of which must be taken together to understand properly what God intends.

1) parental responsibility

2) individual responsibility

It matters a great deal how you rear your children. The doctrine of individual responsibility does not lessen your responsibility as a parent to teach and train your children—it *increases* your responsibility. You must teach them who God is and how to love Him so that, when they are making their own choices, they will want to choose what is right.

You will answer for what you taught your children, and they will answer for what they did with it. Your failure is never an acceptable excuse for their sin. No one is reared in a perfect environment. Train and teach and be an example so that you children will want to make the right choices.

Some people emphasize only the fact that parents are responsible for their children's behavior. They say that Proverbs 22:6 means that if the parents do their job properly, the children will never go astray. However, the doctrine of parental responsibility doesn't free children from responsibility before God for their own actions, and that must also be taken into account.

I know of a preacher whose son went into sin long after he had moved away from home. In fact, the son was in his thirties by the time he went into sin. Nobody called for the pastor to step down from the pulpit. If Proverbs 22:6 means what it is often interpreted as meaning, however, this pastor should have stepped down from his pulpit, because his son's failure, even as an adult, would have been proof that the pastor had not reared his son properly.

Both responsibilities, parental and individual, must be balanced and considered together. So what does Proverbs 22:6 really mean? Years ago I heard a well-known preacher say it means to teach children to go the way they're already going. His emphasis was on training children the way they *would* go rather than the way they *should* go. I think that takes too much away from the Word of God.

Proverbs are general principles. They are always true, but they are not always specifically applicable to every situation. Secular proverbs work the same way. We say, "A stitch in time saves nine." The idea is that if you repair something before it completely breaks, doing so will save you a lot of work. That is true, but it might take seven stitches or twelve stitches to repair a complete rip in a garment, rather than nine. The general truth does not apply exactly the same in each individual case.

The fact that God gives us instruction about rearing children presupposes that following it will have an effect. God does not tell us to do things that don't work. He doesn't give us principles that don't help. How you rear your children does make a difference. It is a generally true principle that if you train them in the way they should go, when they are old, they will not depart from it; but that principle will not override a stubborn will that rebels against God and determines to do its own thing.

There is no magical formula with four steps that guarantee things will turn out the way you want with your children. You'd better get God involved (Ps. 127:1–3). You'd better keep praying. You'd better keep teaching.

I talked to a man once who had six children. They were some of the best children I had ever seen. I said, "What do you do?" He said, "I run scared all the time." I am grateful for the way my daughters have turned out, but something could happen tomorrow that would change their behavior. I don't expect that to happen, but I don't live like it couldn't. I pray for my kids every day.

It is valuable to a pastor's credibility that his children live right.

There are two wrong philosophies when it comes to pastors and their children. I know one preacher who said, "You have to choose—you can either have a great family and not such a great ministry, or you can have a great ministry and not such a great family." He had personally chosen to emphasize his ministry over his family. His children showed the effects of that choice.

I believe that he laid out a false dichotomy. There is no reason that you cannot succeed in both ministry and parenting. It is possible to do what God expects you to do. You do not have to sacrifice your children in order to have an effective ministry.

I know another preacher who said, "If my kids do anything wrong, I'm disqualified from the ministry." I preached for him once a year for a number of years. He had a good church. I watched his kids grow up. When his daughter was fifteen, this man and his wife started to have a problem with her being rebellious. Her mother spanked her, and she ran away to her grandmother's house. The grandmother called Child Protective Services and reported the parents for abuse.

He called me for advice, but said he was going to resign from his church. I told him there was no reason for him to quit. I tried to help and encourage him, but eventually he resigned. He's out of the ministry today. I still see him once in a while, and I'm sad every time I see him. The Bible did not require him to lose his ministry over what happened with his daughter.

It is wrong for a pastor to neglect his children and use the ministry as an excuse.

I don't spend as much time at home as some people do, but my daughters have never felt neglected because I was a pastor. They've never said, "Dad, I hate it that you're gone so much." I've worked to be accessible to them and to make sure they know how important they are to me. I've stayed close to them.

Sometimes people say, "I just have too much to do." God never requires you to neglect one area of responsibility in order to succeed at another. Dr. Bob Jones, Sr., used to say, "Duties never conflict." Of course that doesn't mean that we will never face choices between things that compete to claim our attention, but it does mean that we can do all that God has commanded us to do. He does not give impossible commands.

Children are more likely to follow a parent's heart than his rules.

The problem with a lot of children who go bad is not that they have too many rules. It's usually that Mom and Dad didn't have a really strong relationship with God and/or with each other. Proverbs 23:26 says, "My son, give me thine heart, and let thine eyes observe my ways."

If you want your children to turn out right, the most important

47

thing you can do is win their hearts. I believe in rules. God wants us to teach our children to do right. However, rules without an effective relationship do not produce long-term results.

I hear preacher friends complain sometimes and feel sorry for themselves. Their heart attitude will negatively impact their children. I try to encourage preachers' kids wherever I go. I teach them that preachers' kids are special. I tell them my dad was a preacher, and I share with them the "neat" things I got to do because my dad was a preacher. I like being a preacher's kid because my dad liked being a preacher.

Back in the early 1970s, my dad preached for a church in Detroit, Michigan. They gave him a $1,000 love offering. That's not bad today, but back in those days, it was an enormous gift. My dad was very appreciative of the money. I said, "Wow, Dad. Keep that up and pretty soon you'll be in the big time." Without hesitating, he looked at me and said, "Son, I've been in the big time for twenty years."

My dad was not a perfect father. In the days before cell phones, e-mail and faxes, he would be gone for weeks at a time. I missed him. He worked a lot; but I never doubted he loved me, loved the Lord, and loved the work of the Lord. He made something positive out of everything that happened. He took time to make us feel special. He didn't complain. I caught his heart.

A ruler is not a failure because his subjects fail; he is a failure when he does not deal with their wrongdoing.

A police lieutenant is a member of our church. He's a good police officer. Would it be logical to conclude that if someone in his town breaks the law, he's a failure? Of course not. He would be a failure if he didn't deal with a criminal when he caught him.

We don't hold policemen responsible for crime prevention. Their primary job is law enforcement. Police officers do all that they can to prevent crimes, and they should, but that is not the standard by which their effectiveness is judged. If someone breaks the law, it is their job to deal with him.

The Bible requirement is for a pastor to rule his house well and have his children in subjection. That cannot mean the children never do wrong. Such a requirement could never be met by human beings with a sin nature.

The first disappointed father was God.

Is God a good Father? Do His children always do right? Do our failures in any way reflect on His goodness and righteousness? The fact that all of us sin simply shows our fallen natures. It does not tell us anything about God as a Father.

In the beginning, God created Adam and Eve in a perfect world. They had daily fellowship and communion with Him. Yet Satan successfully tempted Eve, and she and Adam ate the forbidden fruit. God was disappointed in their sin, but He was no less perfect because they fell.

It is possible for a pastor's children to sin so badly that the pastor forfeits his right and ability to serve in a particular place. It is possible for a pastor's children to sin because he has neglected to teach them to do right. Sometimes a pastor neglects his children's lives and needs in order to give his attention to the work of the church. Such a failure may disqualify him from ministry.

Don't judge preachers whose children do wrong. I know some preachers whose children failed terribly: but they loved them and worked with them, and after some time passed, they saw their children come back to God and to their families. One pastor was going to resign from his church because one of his sons had gone into sin. A very wise deacon said to him, "Pastor, if you resign, the rest of us who are struggling with our children won't have an example of how to love them back to God." He stayed on in the ministry, and I believe that was exactly the right thing to do.

A preacher should leave the ministry when his children fail only if he has neglected to train them or neglected to deal properly with them when they sin. That is what the requirement of "ruleth well his own house" means.

CHAPTER SIX
DOES GOD COMMAND THAT ALL GIVING BE DONE SECRETLY?

During my years in the ministry, I've learned that few topics are more sensitive than the topic of money. It seems like people would rather hear a sermon on almost anything other than giving. There are enough jokes about preachers and money to fill several books, but when a pastor preaches or teaches on money, usually people aren't laughing.

Partly because of that sensitivity and partly because of a misinterpretation of some Scripture verses, a teaching has come to be commonly accepted that no one should ever know what one gives. Pastors are advised not to look at giving records, and it is considered a tremendous breach of etiquette for anyone to know what a person has given. There are even some people who refuse to use church offering envelopes because they don't want anyone else to know what they are giving.

THE COMMON TEACHING

This concept that God requires giving always to be done secretly is based on these elements:

God condemns those who give for show.

"Take heed that ye do not your alms before men, to be seen of them: otherwise ye have no reward of your Father which is in heaven.

"Therefore when thou doest thine alms, do not sound a trumpet before thee, as the hypocrites do in the synagogues and in the streets, that they may have glory of men. Verily I say unto you, They have their reward.

51

"But when thou doest alms, let not thy left hand know what thy right hand doeth:

"That thine alms may be in secret: and thy Father which seeth in secret himself shall reward thee openly."—Matt. 6:1–4.

In Bible days, the Pharisees would literally hire someone to sound a trumpet to attract attention when they were going to the temple to give. They were not giving out of a desire to do right, but rather out of a desire to impress others with their generosity and to gain glory for themselves.

God commands us not to let others know what we give.

Jesus said, "That thine alms may be in secret." The people who believe the common teaching about giving use this verse to say that we must always conceal our giving from others.

My family and I were traveling down to Kentucky a few years ago; and since it was Wednesday night, we stopped for church. When we walked in, I noticed that on the end of every aisle there was a pillar with a slot in it that was used for offerings.

When I inquired about these devices, I was informed that this church believed that passing an offering plate violated the Lord's command to give "in secret." I think it's good when people try to obey the Bible, but I believe they were not properly interpreting Scripture.

It's strange to me that we treat giving differently than other aspects of spiritual growth and development. There is nothing unique about giving. It is simply another area in which we are to grow in grace. In a passage about giving, in II Corinthians 8:7, we read, "Therefore as ye abound in every thing, in faith, and utterance, and knowledge, and in all diligence, and in your love to us, see that ye abound in this grace also."

Paul did not treat giving as a separate part of the Christian life. Nobody gets upset when a preacher talks about faith. Nobody gets upset by a message encouraging love. Nobody has a problem with a sermon urging people to study the Word of God and learn more about God's will for their lives. However, when preachers talk about money, many times people react negatively.

Giving is an integral part of our Christian life, but money is so important to so many people that giving gets put into a separate category in our thinking. I think that our general attitude toward money greatly impacts the widespread belief that we should never let anyone know what we give.

THE CONTRADICTORY TRUTH

The Lord condemns both the *method* and the *motive* of ostentatious giving.

Jesus condemned those who give 'sounding a trumpet' and "to be seen of men." He was talking about more than just the method of giving. All through the New Testament, we see that God focuses on heart attitudes, not just on outward behavior. It is not enough to change the method of giving if the motive for giving is not right.

We are very blessed in our church when it comes to the matter of giving. We have some people who can give large amounts of money every year. We have some people who give much smaller amounts, but their sacrifice in giving equals that of some who give the larger gifts.

What we don't have are any really rich people who are big givers. I was preaching for a pastor a few years ago, and he told me, "People think we have money, but we don't. There's only one man in our whole church who gave over a hundred thousand dollars last year." I said, "I'd settle for one!"

Most churches don't have large givers. Studies of philanthropy have shown that most of the people who give hundreds of thousands or even millions of dollars don't tithe to a local church. If you put just your tithe in an offering plate, you won't get a building named after you. You won't receive an honorary doctorate. You won't have a plaque in the foyer of the auditorium.

There are exceptions to the rule, but by and large, people who give large gifts tend to like the attention they receive. Regular giving to the church doesn't satisfy that need. Over the years I've had a lot of people tell me how much they gave to various causes. They want people to know so the people will think well of them. That's not how God wants you to give.

God never commands us not to let others know what we do for Him.

Jesus did say, "Take heed that ye do not your alms before men;"

53

but in the same message—the Sermon on the Mount—He also commanded public good works. Again it's important to realize that God makes no distinction between giving and any of the other things he commands us to do.

God commands us to let others see what we do for Him so that He may be glorified.

Matthew 5:16 says, "Let your light so shine before men, that they may see your good works, and glorify your Father which is in heaven." Part of the confusion regarding giving is caused by the fact that the Hebrew word translated "alms" does not only mean the giving of money. It can be used for any righteous deed. In one part of the sermon, Jesus said, 'Don't do things to be seen by men.' In another place, He said, "Let your light so shine before men." Those statements are not contradictory if you consider that the focus of His warning is on the motivation for the action.

Doing a good deed or giving 'to be seen of men' is the problem—not the doing of good in public. Ananias and Sapphira gave what they represented as the entire purchase price of their property in full view of the church. They made a show of what they were giving because they wanted the approval and praise of men.

They had seen others like Barnabas receive praise for giving, and apparently they wanted that same kind of recognition. It was not announcing their gift that was condemned; it was lying about how much they had received for the sale of their property. The hardest thing in the world to keep right is your motives.

Not long ago, I told a pastor that he ought to check the giving records of his people. He was a little surprised, because he'd been taught the same thing that I had—you weren't supposed to do that. That teaching has no Bible basis. I found that when I reviewed the giving records, I wasn't discouraged. In fact, I was encouraged by how people were giving.

Here's what happened in his church. He said, "When I announced I was going to start looking at the records, the treasurer came and said the offerings were up 23 percent!" While it's not right for people to give to be recognized, it is right for them to give. And it's a good thing for a pastor to encourage people to do right.

No one complains if the pastor asks if a member has been reading his Bible or says that he missed him at a service. I ask people in our church how their prayer lives are. I ask if they're witnessing to others. The Bible says that as a pastor, I have to give an account for them (Heb. 13:17). God holds me responsible to know what's going on in the lives of the members of the First Baptist Church of Bridgeport.

Why should the grace of giving be treated any differently than any of the other graces? The point Jesus was making is not that people should never know what you give. The point is that you shouldn't give—or do any other good work—to be seen of men. You can sing in the choir, teach a Sunday school class, work on a bus route, go out soul winning or give financially either to bring glory to God or to be seen of men.

The question is not *what* you do; it's *why* you do it. Doing something to be seen of men is not just limited to money. Any good work for the Lord can be done with either proper or improper motives.

Paul commended the members of the church at Corinth for their commitment to give. He told them, "Your zeal hath provoked very many" (II Cor. 9:2). Paul told other churches about their eagerness to give, and that motivated others to want to give. That's a good result from a public acknowledgement of giving.

Jesus openly observed what people gave.

"And Jesus sat over against the treasury, and beheld how the people cast money into the treasury: and many that were rich cast in much.

"And there came a certain poor widow, and she threw in two mites, which make a farthing.

"And he called unto him his disciples, and saith unto them, Verily I say unto you, That this poor widow hath cast more in, than all they which have cast into the treasury:

"For all they did cast in of their abundance; but she of her want did cast in all that she had, even all her living."—Mark 12:41–44.

Jesus watched to see how and what people gave. He openly observed while the people were giving. I'm not suggesting that a church should post the members' giving numbers on the back wall of the building. I don't think that would be appropriate because it would probably encourage improper motives for giving. However, if I mention someone's work on a bus route, his soul winning, Bible

55

study or prayer to encourage others, why shouldn't I also be able to mention someone's giving for the same reason?

There are many Bible examples of public giving.

Some years ago we had a special giving campaign for a major project at the church. My pastor friend Dr. Ed Nelson strongly advised me to hire a consultant for the campaign. He said, "They'll want you to do some things that take you out of your comfort zone; and if you're paying them, you'll be more likely to do things that you really need to do to succeed."

One of the things the consultant said was that we needed to have people announce their gifts. My immediate reaction to that was very negative. I had been indoctrinated with the idea that giving should never be public. He pointed me to I Chronicles 29 which describes David's preparation for Solomon to build the temple. David told the people publicly exactly what he personally planned to give for the project (vss. 3–5).

In response to David's example, the people willingly gave to ensure that all of the materials needed for the temple would be in place before the project started (vss. 6–9). Knowing that others around you are committed to the cause has a positive effect on morale and behavior.

When Hernando Cortez invaded Mexico in 1518, he had only a few hundred men to face tens of thousands of Aztec warriors. He knew that if his men had the option of quitting and going home, they might take it when they became discouraged. So before they began their march inland, he burned all their ships. From that point on, they were forced to be committed to succeeding, and each soldier knew his companions were just as committed as he was.

Acts 4:34 tells the story of what happened when there were financial needs in the church at Jerusalem. Many of those who were converted on the day of Pentecost came to Jerusalem from far away. They stayed together in the city. The church in Jerusalem was the only church in the world for a while. They fellowshipped together and learned the teachings of Jesus from the disciples.

Soon some serious needs arose. People who had only planned to stay for a few weeks ran out of money. So those who had land and houses sold them and publicly brought the money. They "laid them down at the apostles' feet" (Acts 4:35). This giving was done in front of the whole church without any rebuke or condemnation.

Paul told the church at Corinth about the giving of the churches at Macedonia. Even out of their deep poverty, they gave liberally and generously (II Cor. 8:1–4). Paul used their giving as an example to inspire the Christians at Corinth to give as well.

THE CONSEQUENCES TAUGHT

We must give with the right motive.

The truth is that the bottom-line motivation for all Christian service is obedience. I heard a preacher say once, "The Lord loves a cheerful giver, but He'll take money from a grouch." It seems from the context that when Paul talked about "cheerful" giving, he was talking about freewill offerings (II Cor. 9:1–11). The Bible doesn't refer to tithing as "giving the tithe." Instead it talks about 'paying tithes' and 'bringing tithes.' The tithe is something we owe to God.

Whether it's tithing or giving, it's important to obey whether or not your heart is right. As God prospers us and prompts us, we should give over and above the tithe. If you don't pay your tithes and give offerings, you have stolen from God (Mal. 3:8, 9). It doesn't matter if you don't feel like it. Try calling up the bank and telling them you're not going to make your car payment this month because you don't feel like you can send it cheerfully. Try that on the mortgage company for your house. Do your duty and obey whether or not you have a good attitude.

While the bottom line of motivation is obedience, the top line is love. The love of Christ constrains us (II Cor. 5:14). There are three motivations for giving. One is **gratitude.** The psalmist asked, "What shall I render unto the LORD for all his benefits toward me?" (Ps. 116:12). He went on to talk about his intention to pay his vows to God in appreciation for all that he had received.

If it cost a million dollars to get saved, it would still be a bargain, yet most of us couldn't afford it; but salvation doesn't cost us anything. In light of what you've received, are you really willing to quibble with God over a few dollars in the offering plate? You could go down a long list of things for which you should be grateful.

In the old Southern Baptist churches, they used to do what they called raising the budget. Everybody would pledge how much he would give for the year.

One year George Truett at the First Baptist Church in Dallas, Texas was conducting the meeting, and they were having trouble raising the money they needed for the coming year. He got a little frustrated and said, "Folks, it's not my church. I don't have the money, and I can't pay the bills. If you don't want to keep it going, I can't do it alone." One man said, "I'm going to give $5,000 in honor of my son who died in the war." Another man nudged his wife and said, "Let's give $10,000 for our son." She said, "Our son didn't die." The man said, "I know. We ought to give more for a son who lived."

We should give for the **glory of God.** When we give, it makes God look good. What a wonderful testimony it is for the world to see God's people giving generously, and what an awful testimony it is when churches can't pay their bills. You ought to do the best you can for God in every area of life, including giving. It glorifies God when we demonstrate that we think He is worthy of our money.

Years ago I read a story in *Reader's Digest* called "Johnny Lingo's Eight Cow Wife." In the culture in which that story was set, a man would pay a certain price for his wife. An average wife would go for one or two cows. A really talented or beautiful wife would go for three or four cows. Johnny Lingo was known as the best trader in the area, so when he agreed to pay eight cows for his wife, everyone was amazed.

The girl he wanted to marry wasn't particularly beautiful, and nobody thought she had anything special to offer. However, her stature in the community skyrocketed because of the price that had been paid for her. Everyone realized how important she was to her husband.

People around us ought to wonder why God is worth so much to us. Giving generously gives us an opportunity to witness.

Finally, we should give to **gain rewards.** Now I know some people respond negatively to that statement. They say that giving for a reward is a carnal motive, but it was God's idea to put that system in place. He said in Proverbs 3:9, 10, "Honour the LORD with thy substance, and with the firstfruits of all thine increase: So shall thy barns be filled with plenty, and thy presses shall burst out with new wine."

Nobody ever ended up poor by honestly and obediently giving to God. Some people may get poor sending money to some guy on television; but it you give the way God designed, you won't get in trouble. Giving does not guarantee financial wealth. The "prosperity gospel" being taught today is a fraud, but God does promise to reward us when we give to Him and His work.

Our gifts should be an example and an encouragement to others.

We've already looked at II Corinthians 8:1 where Paul used the example of the churches of Macedonia to encourage the Corinthians to give. Many years ago I announced in church that I was going to give $80 a week during a stewardship campaign. One man told me later that he determined that night that if I could do that making less than he did, he could give $75 a week. My zeal provoked him to giving.

Again, it's important to realize that the motive for giving should never be to draw attention or praise to ourselves. Proper giving brings glory to God, not to us. Yet giving also does provide us the opportunity to influence others to do right with their finances.

There is no valid reason for us to glory in our giving.

First Corinthians 4:7 says, "For who maketh thee to differ from another? and what hast thou that thou didst not receive? now if thou didst receive it, why dost thou glory, as if thou hadst not received it?" There's an old hymn that doesn't get used very often anymore, but it used to be a common offering song. The words say, "We give Thee but Thine own." I'm glad I get to give. It's a privilege to be part of the work of God, but everything already belongs to Him whether or not we give it to Him (Ps. 24:1).

Dr. John R. Rice used to say, "God wants your money, He wants the wallet your money is in, He wants the pants the wallet is in, and He wants the man in the pants. It all belongs to Him." I don't glory in my giving or in the gift, but in God. My gifts let Him know how much glory I think He deserves.

Allowing giving to be placed in a special "off limits" category instead of understanding it as simply one of the graces of the Christian life has had a negative impact on both churches and individual believers. Recognizing God's plan for our giving allows us to bring glory to Him and receive rewards for our obedience.

CHAPTER SEVEN

ARE WIVES COMMANDED TO LOVE THEIR HUSBANDS?

"Wives, submit yourselves unto your own husbands, as unto the Lord."

"Husbands, love your wives, even as Christ also loved the church, and gave himself for it."—Eph. 5:22, 25.

When I do marital counseling, I tell people that these are the basic commands of Scripture for couples—for husbands to love their wives and for wives to submit to their husbands. This is the foundation of how God planned for marriages to work. Recognizing God as the Creator, we understand that there must be a purpose behind His design. Why did God set up marriage to work this way?

When a wife submits to her husband and when a husband loves his wife, they meet each other's most basic needs. Generally speaking, the most important need a woman has is for security. She needs to know that somebody is completely committed to her. She needs to know that somebody is going to take care of her. She needs to know that somebody is going to love her whether she gets fat or stays skinny, whether her skin is wrinkled or smooth, whether she's having a good day or a bad day. Women need security. God knew that need, so He commanded husbands to love their wives.

Because women need security, they often think men need security too, so they try to make their husbands feel secure. She'll take care of him—by letting him know how to dress, how to behave in public, how to change his manners and how to drive. This kind of woman would like it if someone was as attentive and caring to her as she thinks she's being to her husband.

However, men don't need security. Put us in the middle of a ten-thousand-acre jungle, and we'll find our way out. We'll rub two trees together and start a fire. We'll kill an elephant with rocks. We'll eat dirt if we must. We'll survive. We can make it. That's why we never ask for directions. Men don't need them. Maybe you've heard about Moses wandering in the desert for forty years—and, no, to correct a common misconception, it was *not* just because he wouldn't ask for directions!

A man's most basic need is not security; it is affirmation. It took me 15 or 18 years of ministry to find a more sensitive word for boosting the ego! A man needs somebody to think he's strong and smart and a great leader. When a wife obeys God's command and submits to her husband, she meets his need for affirmation.

Due to the way these foundational commandments are worded in this passage of Scripture, some people have developed a doctrine based on what is *not* said. This contrived doctrine has had a negative impact on families in many good churches.

The Common Teaching

Because Ephesians 5 does not specifically command wives to love their husbands, this doctrine says that Scripture does not command them to do so. The people who hold this belief say that if a husband properly loves his wife, she will automatically love him in return, without needing a commandment to do so. Here is the foundation for this teaching.

Scripture commands husbands to love their wives.

This is unquestionably true. The Bible sets a very high standard for a husband's love: it is to be the same kind of love Christ has for the church (Eph. 5:25). That love is sacrificial, generous, compassionate and more concerned about the other than about self.

Scripture does not command wives to love their husbands.

This is an argument made from silence, which is not a valid way to interpret the Word of God. It is true that such a command is not found in the passage in Ephesians; but we will see, there are other places in Scripture that do say a wife is to love her husband.

If a husband loves his wife as God commands, his wife will automatically love him.

This may be the most damaging part of this teaching. Those who promote it say that if a man is loving his wife as Christ loves the church, it will be automatic for her to love him. This has led to many people's being disappointed and confused about why their marriages are not living up to their expectations.

As we will see, the truth is that wives *are* commanded to love their husbands, and that love is to have the same kind of unconditional basis that husbands are to have in their love for their wives.

THE CONTRADICTORY TRUTH

The Bible commands husband and wife to love each other.

"The aged women likewise, that they be in behaviour as becometh holiness, not false accusers, not given to much wine, teachers of good things;

"That they may teach the young women to be sober, to love their husbands, to love their children,

"To be discreet, chaste, keepers at home, good, obedient to their own husbands, that the word of God be not blasphemed."— Titus 2:3–5.

If the love of a wife for her husband were somehow automatic, there would be no need for the older women to teach the younger women to love their husbands; and it is clear from this passage that wives are to learn to love their husbands.

I was talking to a preacher who believed this common teaching, and I mentioned this passage to him. He said, "Well, it just says that one time." How many times does God have to say something before you should pay attention to it? He expects us to believe and practice everything in His Word.

This passage in Titus commands men to do a number of things, but it does not command men to love their wives. That command has already been given elsewhere in Ephesians 5 and Colossians 3. We need to be faithful to the *whole* counsel of God, not just picking and choosing verses to back up pet doctrines.

God wants a husband and his wife to love each other. Men and women are very different in how they view themselves. There's a reason they sell makeup to women and not to men. Every woman, no matter how beautiful, looks in the mirror and thinks she needs help. In 2004, Dove, the maker of soaps and beauty products, surveyed American women. Only two percent said they thought they were beautiful.

Men don't think that way. "No man ever yet hated his own flesh," the Bible says (Eph. 5:29). Men don't disdain their bodies. In contrast to the Dove study, UCLA surveyed men in America and asked them to place themselves in terms of intelligence and athletic ability among the male population. Ninety percent said they were in the top half, and 50 percent said they were in the top 10 percent!

Regardless of the differences in how men and women think about themselves, there is to be love between a husband and wife. Each needs to learn to understand and express his or her appreciation for the mate God has given and to love that person unconditionally.

Scripture requires all believers to love one another.

First John 4:7 says, "Beloved, let us love one another: for love is of God; and every one that loveth is born of God, and knoweth God." John 13:35 says, "By this shall all men know that ye are my disciples, if ye have love one to another."

Even though the Bible doesn't specifically say in Ephesians 5 that wives are to love their husbands, God's general command to love still applies. By the way, one of the biggest problems with the common teaching is that it can lead a wife to think, *My husband doesn't love me like he's supposed to, so I don't have to love him. If he were doing what he is supposed to, I would automatically love him; but I don't. Therefore, he must be doing something wrong.*

The husband's failure to obey God in loving his wife then becomes an excuse for the wife's failure to obey God in submitting to her husband. That is never the way God wants things to be done. Your obligations to God are not contingent on others' fulfilling their obligations to God.

I got a phone call from a pastor not long ago. He said, "About one-third of our members tithe. The rest give little or nothing." Because I have been in the ministry for a number of years, that didn't come as a surprise to me. Then he said, "Those people who don't tithe are

64

demanding. They want this, and they want that. They want me to be there when they call me. How do you distinguish between those two groups in your treatment of them?"

I said, "I treat them both absolutely the same." The Bible doesn't say the pastor should feed the flock of God who tithe. Besides that, how are they going to learn that if you don't teach them? The obligations that God places on us are between Him and us—never between somebody else and us.

A husband who loves his wife according to the Word of God makes it easier for her to love him but does not guarantee her response.

The Lord does not make us respond as He wants. Jesus said, "O Jerusalem, Jerusalem, thou that killest the prophets, and stonest them which are sent unto thee, how often would I have gathered thy children together, even as a hen gathereth her chickens under her wings, and ye would not!" (Matt. 23:37).

Jesus loved all of His disciples with a perfect love, but that did not make Judas love Him. Because God has given each of us a free will, there is always the possibility that a husband or wife will choose to do wrong, regardless of what his or her spouse does.

I've heard people say, "I've never known of a marriage that had problems where one person was totally at fault." I have. We had a lady who attended our church a number of years ago who had been married to a young man she met at a Christian college. He was actively involved in ministry work and well thought of by the leadership.

At the time they got married, she had no idea that he was a homosexual. He had been counseled very foolishly to get married to "fix his problem." Getting married won't fix any problems you have. If you fail to fix them ahead of time, marriage often makes them worse instead of better.

I tell the young ladies in my church, "Don't ever marry a fixer-upper." Over the years I've learned that girls like mission projects. A girl may think she is going to be the one to change a guy when everyone else has failed. That doesn't work.

In this case, however, the girl did not know ahead of time. They were out in full-time ministry when his sin problem came to light.

65

He left her. I knew that young lady. There wasn't one thing she did to cause his behavior. It wasn't her fault. She did everything she was supposed to do.

Usually problems in a marriage are not just one person's fault, and each mate should take care of his or her faults whether or not the spouse does. You are responsible to God to do right whether or not your mate does right, but it is a false teaching to say that a wife will automatically love her husband if he loves her.

Jonathan Edwards, the famous preacher of the Great Awakening, had a daughter who was beautiful but had a very serious problem with her temper. One day a young man came and asked for her hand in marriage. Edwards said, "No, I will not grant it." The young man said, "You must not think I am worthy of her." Edwards replied, "No, she is not worthy of you." Edwards recognized a character flaw in his daughter that had the potential to make her future husband miserable. Until it was corrected, she was not prepared to be a wife.

THE CONSEQUENCES TAUGHT

Love is a universal obligation of believers.

God requires you to love all Christians. I've heard husbands and wives say, "I just can't feel that way about my spouse." I tell them that love is a behavior. Love is an action. Emotions will often accompany love, but the action of love is what is required and commanded by God.

There are some people who are irritating. One year while I was in college, I stayed for summer school. I thought it would be great to have only one roommate instead of three, but mine was weird. He got up before the rising bell every morning. I'm suspicious of people who get up before they have to do so. He had some pretty strange habits. I was glad when summer was over and I didn't have to room with him anymore.

I didn't like him, but the point is that I'm not commanded to like him. Jonathan Swift said, "Fondness is not within my power, but kindness is." If I love others like God loves me, it doesn't matter to me whether or not they're lovable. I am responsible to love all Christians.

The Bible doctrine of individual soul responsibility teaches that, while we can influence the behavior of others, we cannot guarantee that behavior.

Romans 14:12 says, "So then every one of us shall give account of himself to God." It would not be possible for God to hold us individually accountable if others could force us to behave as they wish.

Do I influence people? Sure. If I didn't believe that, I wouldn't be a pastor. I believe God can change people. The Gospel changes people from being sinners to being saints. I've seen people who were bound by sin and living wicked lives transformed and made happy and free in Christ.

However, I cannot change people. If I could, that would put me in charge of their lives, and they would not have to answer directly to God. While people can be helped, they cannot be forced to change. Their response cannot be guaranteed. So many times people feel like they are to blame because their spouses did not do right.

The fact that a husband loves his wife does not guarantee that she will love him. The fact that a wife submits to her husband does not guarantee that he will love her. Our job is to do our part by our words and actions to influence others to do right and leave the outcome up to God.

John Quincy Adams, the sixth president, was defeated by Andrew Jackson when he ran for reelection. Rather than sinking into depression, he returned home and ran for Congress. He served as a representative from Massachusetts, helping to lead the fight in Congress to abolish slavery.

Adams was asked once if he was discouraged because so little progress was being made on the difficult issue. He replied, "Duties are ours; results are God's." There is a tremendous peace in leaving the outcome in God's hands rather than taking responsibility for things we cannot control.

When someone makes a dogmatic statement unsupported by Scripture, we need to check it out carefully.

Many errors and commonly believed false teachings gain acceptance because people fail to compare what is being taught to

67

the Word of God. Even if the teachers are widely respected and looked up to, they may be saying some things that aren't so.

I was in a meeting once where a pastor was teaching on justice. I was taking notes. He said, "If I didn't see him do it or he doesn't tell me he did it, then I do not know that he did it." I wrote down what he said. Next to it, I wrote, "Not biblical." Deuteronomy 19:15 says, "One witness shall not rise up against a man for any iniquity, or for any sin, in any sin that he sinneth: at the mouth of two witnesses, or at the mouth of three witnesses, shall the matter be established."

That pastor who was teaching on justice was a good man who helped me in many areas of the ministry. He encouraged me in many ways. But his teaching on that issue not only was not supported by Scripture, it was directly contradicted by Scripture. If I had accepted his teaching without comparing it to the Word of God, I would have believed something that was not true.

Most decent people, when they are confronted with something they have done wrong, will admit it. They may only let out part of the truth at a time, but good and honorable people will confess. There are some other people who will never admit the truth. With witnesses, God has established a way to find the truth even concerning people like that.

Another time I heard a preacher say, "There will never be a nationwide revival. We're living in an age of apostasy, and God never sends revival during apostasy." That statement at first glance sounds logical, but it's not in the Bible. In fact, if you study revivals in the Word of God, apostasy is not a reason you can't have revival—it is *the* reason you need to have revival.

Israel was far gone from God when they found the Book of the Law in the days of Josiah (II Kings 22:8). God sent revival in that time of apostasy (II Kings 23). If that man who was speaking about apostasy and revival had used a verse or a principle from Scripture to back up his statement, it would have been different; but he just made a flat statement. He was an impressive speaker and a good friend of mine, but he said something that wasn't true.

In contrast, when Paul preached in the city of Berea those who heard him compared what he said to the Word of God. Acts 17:11 says, "These were more noble than those in Thessalonica, in that they received the word with all readiness of mind, and searched the scriptures daily, whether those things were so."

The word that is translated "searched" in our English Bible was used in the Greek legal system to describe the gathering of evidence. It indicates a careful study to determine what is true and what is false. In every area—whether it relates to marriage or to something else—we need to be wary of those who make declarative statements unsupported by Scripture. Such statements are not automatically false, but neither do they deserve unquestioning support.

Chapter Eight
Is It Legalistic to Have Standards?

A while back someone gave me a tape by Dr. John MacArthur and asked me to listen to it. MacArthur, who is pastor of a large church in Southern California, is a best-selling author and has a widely heard daily radio program. He holds rallies around the country and encourages other pastors to follow his philosophies of ministry.

In the message he said, "Well, there are people who tell you that if you take weeds and cut them up and wrap them up in a piece of paper and burn them, that's a sin." His congregation laughed. "There are people who say if you play cards it's a sin." He named other things like drinking and going to movies. All the things he mentioned are things that I preach against. The people listening apparently thought it was funny that anyone would think those things are wrong.

Late one night as I was driving home from a meeting I heard Charles Swindoll, another popular teacher, on the radio. He was trying to teach young people to be morally pure. Now that's certainly a worthy message. He said, "I know it's hard. I know you go to movies and you see things that make you burn, but try to do right."

I preached back to the radio right there in the car. I said, "Tell them not to go there in the first place!" If going to a place makes you want to do wrong, you shouldn't go there. That seems like a pretty simple concept, doesn't it?

There's a strong element in "popular Christianity" today that says, "You can't tell people how to live. You can't infringe on their liberty by telling them not to drink or smoke; that's their decision. You can't make decisions for people." That philosophy is creeping into fundamental churches as well.

The standards concerning righteous living which I believe and preach were widely practiced by fundamentalists until recent times. Many people have now switched over to what the liberals believed back then. That isn't because the Bible has changed. People have been led astray by smooth talkers teaching a false concept of grace and Christian liberty.

The Common Teaching

This kind of teaching is based on the following principles:

Christians answer to God and not to man.

Like most popular false teachings, this statement is based on a partial truth. Romans 14:12 says, "So then every one of us shall give account of himself to God." It is certainly true that we are individually responsible to God. Each of us must ultimately face Him for an assessment of his behavior and motives (II Cor. 5:10).

Most of the commonly disputed areas of behavior are not specifically mentioned in the Bible.

This is a true statement as well. The Bible doesn't say anything about reading *Playboy* or watching MTV. It doesn't condemn the latest dance craze by name. It doesn't say anything about heavy metal or rap music. It doesn't say, "Thou shalt not attend a movie." It doesn't address by commandment many of today's issues.

In these matters Christians have liberty to decide for themselves.

Realizing that this statement might be challenged, frequently proponents of this view will cite verses like, "Let every man be fully persuaded in his own mind" (Rom. 14:5). The danger with this teaching is that it is very easy for it to degenerate into, "If it feels good, do it." As we examine the biblical concept of liberty, we will find there is a stark contrast between it and this teaching.

It is wrong for leaders to set standards or make people feel guilty about their behavior in these areas.

They say that preaching and teaching on standards is putting people on a guilt trip. Frequently those of us who believe in stand-

72

ards are accused of promoting a performance-based theology. They say, "God doesn't love you because of what you do; God loves you because of who you are."

That is true, but it's irrelevant to the discussion of standards. God loves sinners and sent Jesus to die for us before we were born. God loves us because He is love, not because of anything we do or don't do. It is equally true, however, that God gives us certain standards of behavior and blesses us as we obey Him in those areas.

A man who was involved in a Christian ministry told his kids, "You don't have to listen to anything your teacher says if it's 'performance-based acceptance.'" When I heard about that, I said, "He doesn't really believe that. He wouldn't say to his future son-in-law, 'I love you no matter how you treat my daughter. I'll feel the same whether you beat her or kiss her.'"

He has standards for what kind of performance is acceptable, whether or not he's willing to accept the standards of others.

THE CONTRADICTORY TRUTH

A careful study of Scripture reveals the problems with teaching that it is legalistic to expect certain standards of behavior.

Christians are to obey God *and* man.

What these people who oppose having standards do is to take a partial truth and pretend that it's the whole truth. Yes, Christians do answer to God, but there are also areas in which we have an obligation to answer to the authorities God has placed over us. In I Corinthians 11:1, Paul said, "Be ye followers of me, even as I also am of Christ."

The Bible teaches the principle of obedience to earthly authority in both secular and spiritual matters. Wives are to be in submission to their husbands (Col. 3:18). Children are to be obedient to their parents (Col. 3:20). Servants are to obey their masters (Col. 3:22). All of us are to obey civil authorities (Rom. 13:1, 2).

It is a false teaching to say, "I answer *only* to God." I knew of a secretary in a church who said she didn't want to do what the preacher told her to do because she worked for God, not him. It was a ministry, and she was going to do what she thought God wanted her to do. I think it's more than a little ironic that she still expected to be paid by the church even though she didn't want to follow its leader.

God's order throughout Scripture is that there are human leaders to guide His people and carry out His program. Picture in your mind a fifteen year-old boy who says, "My parents didn't want me to go out shopping with my friends, but I prayed about it and felt God wanted me to go. I may meet somebody I can witness to or somebody who really needs help."

Anyone who lives that way cannot be right with God. We cannot substitute our emotions or feelings for obedience to the authorities God has placed in our lives. Christians answer to both God and man.

Liberty is not license to do wrong.

It's interesting how the people who teach against standards pick and choose verses. They tend to focus on the ones that seem to back up their point and ignore the rest. Galatians 5:1 says, "Stand fast therefore in the liberty wherewith Christ hath made us free, and be not entangled again with the yoke of bondage." This verse is frequently used by those who oppose standards, but they do not consider the complete context.

If you read the full passage, you come to verse 13 which says, "For, brethren, ye have been called unto liberty; only use not liberty for an occasion to the flesh, but by love serve one another." It is clear that the liberty in verse 1 is not the liberty to do anything we want.

We hear a lot about grace from those teaching against standards. They say that those of us who believe there are some things God's children shouldn't do, just don't understand or believe in grace. Again if we allow Scripture to define *grace,* we get a very different picture.

"For the grace of God that bringeth salvation hath appeared to all men,

"Teaching us that, denying ungodliness and worldly lusts, we should live soberly, righteously, and godly, in this present world."— Titus 2:11, 12.

Paul told Titus that grace teaches us to live, not in any manner we choose, but in a holy and godly manner as a testimony to the lost

74

world around us. Jude talked about men who 'turn the grace of God into lasciviousness' (Jude 4).

Liberty in the Bible is always liberty to do what is right. Liberty is freedom from bondage to sin and the world. It allows us to follow the commands of God and live a life that is pleasing to Him.

Here is where the opponents of standards go astray. They cite what is true about salvation and try to apply it to discipleship. Some of these same people also cite the verses about discipleship and try to apply them to salvation. They say that before a person can be saved he must submit to the Lordship of Christ. The Lordship of Christ is a doctrine for believers, which governs how we are to live.

They cite verses like the ones in Galatians 5 that are in reference to salvation and misapply them. Here is the fact of the matter. You are saved by grace. If you add the law to grace as a requirement for salvation, then you are truly a legalist. The people who think there is a requirement to keep the law to get saved are what the Bible calls legalists.

The scriptural definition of legalism is adding something to faith in Christ either to get saved or to stay saved. When Paul asked the Galatians, "Having begun in the Spirit, are ye now made perfect in the flesh?" he was not talking about Christian living. He was talking about completing the work of salvation. Eternal security is not achieved through keeping rules.

There is no Bible standard of behavior for staying saved. To get saved, you have to "believe on the Lord Jesus Christ" (Acts 16:31). Once you are saved, you are God's child. If you go to movies, get drunk, commit adultery, lie, steal or murder somebody, you're still saved.

The Bible is filled with examples of this. Peter was a saved man when he denied the Lord Jesus. That didn't make him lost. Jesus didn't come to Peter on the shore of lake Galilee and witness to him. Instead, Jesus restored Peter to a loving relationship with Himself (John 21:15–22).

Eternal security does not mean, however, that God doesn't care how you live after you're saved. Liberty is not license to do wrong.

God sets standards.

In both the Old and New Testaments, there are guidelines for behavior. Deuteronomy 22:8 says, "When thou buildest a new house, then thou shalt make a battlement for thy roof, that thou bring not blood upon thine house, if any man fall from thence." In Bible times, houses had flat roofs. Where I pastor in Michigan, you don't ever see a flat roof. With the snowfall here, the weight would crush the roof if it were not slanted so most of the snow falls off. That was not a problem in the Holy Land.

Steps outside the house would go up to the roof. It would be cooler up there in the evenings with a breeze, and often the people would sit there to relax at the end of the day. God told the people to put a battlement—a guardrail—around the roof. That way the homeowner would not be responsible if someone fell off the roof.

Could you still fall off a roof even with a guardrail? Sure. Could you avoid falling off a roof without a guardrail? Sure; but the principle is that there needs to be protection. For that same reason we have a railing around the balcony at our church. It's a practical thing to make it safer for people.

That's what standards are—practical protective devices to keep you safe. God went on to give the Israelites other guidelines for their behavior. "Thou shalt not sow thy vineyard with divers seeds" (vs. 9). "Thou shalt not plow with an ox and an ass together" (vs. 10). "Thou shalt not wear a garment of divers sorts, as of woollen and linen together" (vs. 11).

Why did God issue those instructions? These rules which God gave the Israelites are what we call ceremonial law. They governed the nation of Israel, but they are not binding on Christians today. The Bible says Jesus blotted out "the handwriting of ordinances that was against us" when He died on the cross (Col. 2:14). Any moral law which is repeated in the New Testament is still binding today.

Why did God issue these very specific rules to the Israelites? God wanted to teach them a principle. He wanted it to be acted out in daily life. It is the great principle of separation. God has always been a separatist. Even creation began with a division of light and darkness (Gen. 1:4).

All through the day the Israelites would be reminded of this principle. As they got dressed, they could not put on a garment made of two different fabrics. As they hitched up their team to plow the field, they could not hitch an ox and a donkey in the same harness; as they planted the seeds, they could not sow two kinds of seed in the same field. God wants an obvious difference between His people and the world.

The truth is, the Jews would have been no less godly for wearing blended fabrics, plowing with a mixed team or planting mixed seed—except that God wanted them to meet that standard. It illustrated the principle of separation, and God commanded their obedience. Because of the principle of separation, God set up a standard that otherwise had nothing to do with issues of right and wrong.

A principle is a Bible truth I must live by. A conviction is a personal belief based on a principle. A standard is a guideline to help keep the conviction. To illustrate that, let me show you how the process works.

- The principle—"I will set no wicked thing before mine eyes" (Ps. 101:3).
- The conviction (based on the principle)—I shouldn't read or view pornography.
- The standard—I won't knowingly walk down the aisle of the grocery store where they sell the wrong kind of magazines.

Following standards helps me keep my convictions and obey Bible principles. The issue isn't seeds, fabrics or animals. The issue is separation. God wanted His people to follow the standards so they would understand the principle.

We see the same thing in the New Testament. In Acts 15 we have the record of a church council being held in Jerusalem. Once the missionary work began in earnest, problems arose because some of the converts were Jews and some were Gentiles. There have always been divisions because of ethnicity and background. The things that unite us in Christ are greater than anything that would divide us. We are all one in Him; but because of sinful human natures, we still have conflicts at times.

The Jewish converts thought the Gentile converts should obey the law the same way they did. They saw these new believers doing things they thought were wrong. They wanted the church leadership to enforce their rules on the Gentile believers. They thought the Gentile Christians were a bad influence and an embarrassment.

James issued this instruction: "Wherefore my sentence is, that we trouble not them, which from among the Gentiles are turned to

God" (vs. 19). There are two great principles here that are badly needed in fundamental circles today.

First, the church leaders told the Jewish believers, "If it violates your conscience, don't do it; but don't force your rules on everybody else."

Second, they instructed the Gentile believers to follow certain guidelines to keep peace. I believe if we got back to being truly "independent," we would not try to make everybody else do things our way. But all of us should also be willing to go to great lengths not to offend.

There are four items on the list James issued as guidelines for the Gentile believers. Abstaining from "pollutions of idols" and abstaining from "fornication" are moral issues. Abstaining from "things strangled" and abstaining from "blood" are not moral issues (vs. 20). It is fully appropriate for New Testament Christians to have standards in both moral and nonmoral matters.

The church leaders set a standard which included some items that were not moral issues in order to keep peace in the church. It was for everybody's benefit for them to keep those standards. The Gentiles were asked to accommodate their Jewish brethren to keep from causing offense and making others stumble. We are not to do anything that would damage the life of a weaker brother.

I was once invited to preach for a man who believes that preachers should always wear white shirts. It is a big deal to him. The schedule hasn't worked out yet for me to go, but if I ever preach for him, I'll wear a white shirt. I don't hold that standard, but not causing an offense is worth more than wearing a blue shirt.

I learned that principle from my father when I was a teenager. There was a man who lived across the street from my family who worked for the city of Royal Oak in the daytime, and he was also a part-time Zion Wesleyan Holiness preacher. His wife didn't wear jewelry or makeup. She never cut her hair. Neither the men nor the women in that church would wear short-sleeved shirts, even in the heat of summer.

They were *very* separated. He invited me to attend a revival service they had, and I got my dad's permission to go. As I was getting ready to go to church, I got out a nice pair of slacks and a blue short-sleeved shirt. It was the middle of July, and it was hot.

My dad said, "Where are you going?" I said, "To church with our neighbors." He said, "Not in that shirt, you're not." I said, "We don't believe it's wrong to wear short-sleeved shirts." He replied, "They do; and you're going to their church, and you're going as their guest. Go put on a long-sleeved shirt."

He was saying that there are some things that may not be sinful that you shouldn't do in order not to offend others. It is worth giving up part of your freedom to keep peace in the body of Christ.

Bible principles cannot be applied in the absence of standards.

By way of example, let's look at one of the most contentious areas of standards—clothing. Why do we teach Christian people about how they dress? What are the underlying principles? Modesty and testimony. Almost nobody on either side of the standards argument would contest that. There is a clear Bible principle about the importance of modesty in dress (I Tim. 2:9).

However, the principle in isolation has no meaning. Why do we have speed limits? What's the principle? Safety and protection. Why don't they take down the red lights and stop signs and replace them with reminders to "Be Safe"?

"If we'd all just drive safely, we wouldn't need these legalistic traffic laws," I can hear someone say; but the principle alone is not enough. You cannot apply the principle of safety without some kind of standards. Someone must take the responsibility to say, "This is as fast as you can go on this road. You have to stop here when you come to the intersection."

If you stop and think about it, traffic standards are very arbitrary. Have you ever seen a speed limit of 27, 32, 54 or 68? Speed limits on public highways are set in multiples of five. Do you really think the very fastest you could safely go is 25? Wouldn't it be more scientific if they had said 27.4 mph? Speed limits represent arbitrary choices, but they are important.

To a certain degree, so are our standards. I can't prove to you from Scripture that a man's hair should be cut off his ears. I can prove that a man shouldn't have long hair. We set a standard that we thought was safe. I can't prove to you from the Bible that a lady's dress should come to her knees, but I can prove that a woman is scripturally obligated to be modest.

We have to draw a line somewhere. A certain set of standards is essential for the application of principles. That's what the church leaders set up in Acts 15 when they issued guidelines for Gentile believers.

God gives human leaders the responsibility to establish standards of behavior.

Ephesians 6:1 does not say, "Children obey your parents as long as their rules conform exactly to your understanding of Scripture and they can cite clear Bible verses that demonstrate the need for every standard." The command for obedience is not based on understanding or agreement. It is absolute.

I can't prove to my children from the Bible what their bedtime should be. I can't prove to them that it's wrong for them to wear some items of clothing that are like what other children wear. I can prove to them that they are supposed to do what I say.

The same principle holds true in a church setting. Hebrews 13:17 says, "Obey them that have the rule over you, and submit yourselves: for they watch for your souls, as they that must give account, that they may do it with joy, and not with grief: for that is unprofitable for you."

God's Word tells us that in the church we are to follow the guidance of our spiritual leaders. I can't prove to you from the Bible that every standard we have set in place is exactly what it should be. I can tell you that to the best of our ability, every one of those standards is there because we're trying to obey the principles of Scripture.

There are many issues that are difficult. Good, godly people disagree on some matters. Recently two music directors were talking about music. They were disagreeing about two songs. Each had one song he would do that the other wouldn't, and vice versa. Both these men had gone to the same college. Each earned a master's degree from the same college. They both work in independent, fundamental, Baptist churches. The difference between them is primarily a matter of taste, not a matter of right and wrong.

I may get to Heaven and find out that a song I didn't approve for the choir would have been okay. Somewhere I have to draw a line. God places that responsibility on the pastor. I will tell you that my guideline is to err on the side of caution. I don't insist that the people in our church agree with my reasoning and judgment on every decision, but I do insist that the music meet the standards we have put in place.

There is safety in following the standards of leadership. I've had people say to me, "I don't see what's wrong with going to movies." My reply is, "I don't see what's wrong with not going to movies." How does it hurt your Christian life and witness not to go? How does it make you be a worse Christian?

I've been pastor of the First Baptist Church of Bridgeport for thirty years. I've never yet had a person say to me, "If only I had gone to the movies, I'd be so much closer to God. I wouldn't be in this backslidden condition today." I have had some people who have told me in counseling sessions that they went to movies and saw things they shouldn't have seen and they had a negative impact on their spiritual life and walk with God.

THE CONSEQUENCES TAUGHT

Be extremely wary of those who ridicule the concept of standards.

Don't make fun of or look down on people whose standards are different from yours. The natural tendency is to think anyone with standards lower than yours is a liberal compromiser and anyone with standards higher than yours is a Pharisee, but the Bible says that kind of thinking is foolish.

"For we dare not make ourselves of the number, or compare ourselves with some that commend themselves: but they measuring themselves by themselves, and comparing themselves among themselves, are not wise."—II Cor. 10:12.

Several years ago I preached at two churches that were fairly close together. The pastor of the first church told me the other church didn't have very good standards. I asked what he meant, and he said they had mixed swimming activities for the teenagers. The pastor of the second church told me the other church didn't have very good standards. I asked him what he meant, and he said that their music standards weren't very strong.

Each of those pastors was convinced that the other one was wrong and that his own church was better because there was something on which he had a higher standard than the other one. I kept

81

it to myself, but I thought our church was really good, because we didn't have a problem in either of those areas!

Don't make the mistake of assuming you are more spiritual because you have standards that are higher than someone else's. That was the flaw in the Pharisee's thinking (Luke 18:10–14). Don't make the mistake of thinking that someone with standards higher than yours is an object of ridicule. Be cautious of people who make a mockery of standards.

Standards don't make you spiritual. Standards are guidelines to keep you safe and help you obey God. Spirituality only comes as a result of your relationship with Jesus Christ. I know some Christians who have lots of standards but are as mean as the Devil. They're ungodly and rotten. If you don't go back to the principle but just have the rules that are taught by the institution, the Devil will sneak in something that will get you eventually.

I have a pastor friend who has really high standards. In some areas his standards are higher than mine. Years ago he began having a holiness conference in his church. Another well-known Christian leader said rather sarcastically, "Now I have to go there and learn how to be holy." He didn't like the standards of my friend and was critical of how they did things.

My friend has had a number of people say all kinds of things about him that aren't true. Somebody made a fairly critical comment about him to me once, and I said, "They have a great church. They're getting things done for God. People are being saved, and the church is growing. Why would I be critical of them for wanting to be holy and trying to do right?"

I have pastor friends who don't believe anybody should own a television. I don't think it's a sin to have a television if it's controlled, but I don't make fun of those men for having stricter standards than I have. It shouldn't make you nervous if somebody has higher standards than you. Ask him why he believes that standard. Maybe God will use him to teach you something that will help you grow closer to Him.

Don't think people are rotten if they don't have all the same standards you do. Don't be a Pharisee. If you're not careful, you'll treat others like the New Evangelicals treat fundamentalists.

We should develop personal standards based on Bible principles.

We talked earlier about the responsibility God places on leaders to set standards, but one of the cardinal doctrines of Baptists is the individual priesthood of the believer. God holds you personally accountable for your walk with Him.

I preached a series on standards in our church a few years ago. I didn't spend my time trying to defend my standards. I spent a lot of time trying to teach the principles from Scripture that God expects us to follow. My goal was to get the people of our church to make decisions regarding their own standards based on God's Word. I want them to know the reasons, not just the regulations.

If your personal standards are higher than those of leadership, follow yours; if the leader's standards are higher, follow his.

There are people in my church who will not go into any establishment where alcohol is served. I don't have that standard for my own life. Sometimes I go to restaurants that serve liquor. I don't drink alcohol in any amount at any time, but I will eat there. However, to those people who have that standard I say, "God bless you. You shouldn't ever go to a place that serves liquor." I don't want them to lower their standards.

There are some people who object very strongly to buying anything in a church building. They don't believe a church should have a bookstore. I don't have that standard for our church. We have a bookstore. To those people, however, I say, "Don't buy anything in our bookstore."

I respect people who live by what they believe, even if I disagree with them on some point. I don't try to change them to make them agree with me. Don't just be what everybody around you is; be what you believe God wants you to be.

I don't think the people who condemn having standards are honest or fair in their teaching. They do have some standards. Even the wildest of them draw lines somewhere. They disagree about where the lines are drawn, but instead of admitting that is the area of disagreement, they pretend they don't have standards and call those who do legalists.

There is safety in following high standards. I would much prefer to be a little too strict and stay safe than to risk a disaster by trying to push the boundaries of what is acceptable. There is ample example in the Word of God for standards in both moral and nonmoral areas. You are wise to take the time to study Scripture and develop standards for your life, and then live by them.

CHAPTER NINE

DOES GOD CARE ONLY ABOUT THE HEART?

In the Christian world today, there is a great deal of controversy over whether or not we should have standards for dress and appearance. On the side of those who oppose such standards, a teaching has arisen that, since God looks on the heart of man, the outward appearance should not matter.

One of the primary verses used to support this teaching is I Samuel 16:7: "But the LORD said unto Samuel, Look not on his countenance, or on the height of his stature; because I have refused him: for the LORD seeth not as man seeth; for man looketh on the outward appearance, but the LORD looketh on the heart." From that verse and others like it, they draw these conclusions.

THE COMMON TEACHING

The Bible is very clear that God does examine the thoughts, motives and intentions of our heart. Hebrews 4:12 says, "For the word of God is quick, and powerful, and sharper than any twoedged sword, piercing even to the dividing asunder of soul and spirit, and of the joints and marrow, and is a discerner [revealer] of the thoughts and intents of the heart."

God looks on the heart.

God sees and knows everything, even that which is hidden to man. The psalmist said,

"O LORD, thou hast searched me, and known me.

"Thou knowest my downsitting and mine uprising, thou understandest my thought afar off."—Ps. 139:1, 2.

In His omniscience, God is constantly evaluating what is going on in our hearts.

Man looks on the outward appearance.

We have nothing else to go by. We don't have the ability to determine for certain what is going on inside someone else's heart. His countenance may reveal his heart, but sometimes we're mistaken in our perception of someone's feelings.

A very well-known evangelist came to our church years ago and preached in chapel at our Christian school. He thought one of the girls was making fun of him while he was preaching. After he preached, he told me, "That girl has been looking at me scornfully during this entire sermon." I found out who it was and was surprised to hear it, because we'd never had any trouble with her.

The next day it happened again. It got to him a little bit. In fact, he said that if she did it the third day, he was going to call her down publicly. The girl was a fine girl. She was a model student. I had never seen a negative spirit reflected on her face. I went to her and asked what was going on. She didn't have a problem at all. He had simply misinterpreted her expressions, wrongly thinking she was being critical of his preaching.

The heart is very important.

Up to this point, the teaching is entirely correct and in line with the Word of God. The heart does matter a great deal. Proverbs 4:23 says, "Keep thy heart with all diligence; for out of it are the issues of life." God expects and commands that we keep Him in first place in our hearts (Matt. 22:37).

Therefore, the outward appearance is irrelevant.

This is where the teaching departs from Scripture. While it is true that God looks at the heart, that does not mean in any way that the outward appearance is not important. Sometimes a person will ask, "Why do you judge me just because of the way I look?" The truth is that everyone makes judgments based on appearance.

It is true that there are people who have a good heart whose looks may not meet our standards. One of the good men on our church staff, Brother Swain, had long hair when he got saved. He didn't cut his hair for eight months. His heart was good, and he loved the Lord, but he hadn't been fully educated yet. He finally cut his hair for a job interview. The change in his appearance signaled a change in his spiritual maturity, not in his heart toward God.

I'd be pleased if none of the ladies in our church ever wore slacks again, but the truth is that I know some good Christian ladies who wear slacks. My wife's grandmother was one of the best Christians I've ever met. She had a heart for God. When she got old and couldn't go out and witness, she'd pray for people to call her number accidentally so she would have an opportunity to win people to Christ.

She decided waiting for people to call was too slow, so she started going through the phone book in Kissimmee, Florida, calling people and witnessing to them. She was always learning truth from the Word of God.

She wore pants.

I've also known some ladies who always wore dresses but were mean and judgmental and didn't display any of the fruits of the Spirit in their lives.

Some people who don't have what I would consider to be the best appearance on the outside, do have a great heart. As a result, some people believe there is no need to worry about the outside at all. "Just make sure your heart is right," they say. To them, hair and clothes and appearance don't matter.

God deals with His children at different times about different things. If someone who doesn't look like us comes to our church, our people go up, shake hands with him and say, "We're glad you're here. God bless you." That doesn't mean that we approve of everything about that person's appearance, but we are responsible to give acceptance even when we cannot give approval.

I heard about a lady who went to a church in the Midwest and was told by one of the leading ladies in the church, "Don't come in here wearing pants." What a tragedy it is to refuse people based on their failure to measure up to our standards. What is a church for if it is not a place where people can grow spiritually?

THE CONTRADICTORY TRUTH

God commands us to be right on the inside.

We have already looked at the admonition of Proverbs 4:23 that we must carefully guard our hearts. That's because it is impossible to be righteous from the outside in. You will always fail if you try to do it that way. God's plan is for His children to be right from the inside out.

One of the reasons that Brother Swain eventually cut his hair is that God had been working on his heart. A foundation was being laid for obedience to God.

You do what you do on the outside because of who you are on the inside. I've had people sit in my office and say, "Well, I'm not really like that. I was just under pressure that day." I know that there are times of pressure that cause us to react worse than we normally would, but the reason that bad things come out when you're under pressure is that they were inside in the first place. If you squeeze an orange, you don't get grape juice. You get orange juice because that is what's inside an orange. A wrong heart will sooner or later demonstrate itself outwardly.

Dr. Bob Jones, Sr., used to say, "Behind every tragedy of human character is a long process of wicked thinking." If we allow wrong thoughts and attitudes to linger, they will begin to influence our behavior. God wants our hearts to be right toward Him.

God also instructs His people concerning their outward appearance.

"And the LORD spake unto Moses, saying,

"Speak unto the children of Israel, and bid them that they make them fringes in the borders of their garments throughout their generations, and that they put upon the fringe of the borders a ribband of blue:

"And it shall be unto you for a fringe, that ye may look upon it, and remember all the commandments of the LORD, and do them; and that ye seek not after your own heart and your own eyes, after which ye use to go a whoring:

"That ye may remember, and do all my commandments, and be holy unto your God.

"I am the LORD your God, which brought you out of the land of Egypt, to be your God: I am the LORD your God."—Num. 15:37–41.

God's instruction for His people was for there to be a visible reminder of His commandments on their clothing. If you see an orthodox Jew even today, there will be a fringe somewhere on his garments. He still observes that instruction of God concerning the outward appearance.

This commandment was given to the nation of Israel. It was part of the ceremonial law that governed their behavior. It is not binding on us today, but there is a principle that is illustrated by this commandment that is for us—our outward appearance does matter to God.

Those teachers who use I Samuel 16:7 to support this common teaching aren't examining the context carefully. If you were to ask most of them about whom God was talking when He said that, they would answer that it was David. He was the youngest. He was short and sunburned. So most people would say God was using David as an example to show we should not judge people because they don't measure up on the outside.

I didn't fully realize this at first, but now I see that's completely wrong. Samuel was not referring to David in this verse; he was referring to Eliab. He thought that Eliab, Jesse's oldest son, was the one God had chosen to be the king because he was so physically impressive. Samuel was so impressed with Eliab's appearance that he was certain that God had selected him.

First Samuel 16:7 is not talking about a man who looked bad on the outside but had a good heart. It refers to a man who looked good on the outside but didn't measure up inside. The common teaching uses that verse to support a doctrine that is exactly opposite of what God intended.

God was talking about the error of thinking someone is good because of his outward appearance. Eliab looked good to Samuel, but God was not impressed. There is no such statement made about David. David also had a beautiful countenance (vs. 12), but it was his heart that caused God to select him.

Eliab's heart problem shows up in I Samuel 17. He was in the army, while David was not. Yet David had the faith in God to stand up against Goliath. Eliab failed the test. He was critical of David. He was angry that David wanted to stand up to the giant. Eliab falsely accused David of having wrong motives for what he was doing.

In every interaction and conversation recorded in I Samuel 16 and 17, David honored God. He was obedient to his father. He had faith in God. He stood up for what was right. He did not respond with anger when he was falsely accused. His heart was focused on God. It was because his heart was right that God chose David to be the next king of Israel.

THE CONSEQUENCES TAUGHT

God cares about *both* the outside and the inside.

1) A proper outside appearance is a requirement. First Corinthians 11:14 says, "Doth not even nature itself teach you, that, if a man have long hair, it is a shame unto him?" God has certain standards that He has given us to maintain regarding our appearance. One of those standards is that God wants there to be a visible difference between men and women. I think you ought to be able to tell the difference between genders whether they're coming or going.

We have standards and guidelines for people in our church. I'm not sure that every one is exactly right. We might be off half an inch on one of them. I may get to Heaven and find out that men's sideburns could have been longer than we allowed them to be, but we have made the decision to err on the side of caution to make sure the distinctive is maintained. As far as we know, we are obeying the requirement God has for us as His children.

2) The outside appearance is a revelation. Genesis 31:2 says, "And Jacob beheld the countenance of Laban, and, behold, it was not toward him as before." Laban's face revealed that his heart had changed toward Jacob. What was in his heart showed on the outside. Laban didn't tell Jacob of his feelings, but they showed.

A few years ago, there was a sweet family in our church. All of a sudden things changed. The husband wouldn't shake my hand at church. I immediately started asking around to see if I had done something to upset them. It turned out that they had gotten one of our staff members a Bible for his birthday. When he opened the package, he said, "I knew you were going to give me this Bible. They asked how he knew, and he told them I had informed him what his present would be. He was just kidding with them. I knew nothing about the gift before or after it was given until I learned they were upset, but they took his teasing seriously. They were upset with me because they thought I had ruined their surprise, and their inward displeasure showed on their faces and in their outward behavior.

3) The outside appearance is a reflection. Exodus 34:29 says, "And it came to pass, when Moses came down from mount Sinai with the two tables of testimony in Moses' hand, when he came down from the mount, that Moses wist not that the skin of his face shone while he talked with him." Moses' face shone because he had been with God. He had been exposed to the glory of God, and it showed.

There is a similar story in the New Testament. When Stephen was brought to trial before the Sanhedrin, "all that sat in the council, looking stedfastly on him, saw his face as it had been the face of an angel" (Acts 6:15).

The outward things in our lives—the way we dress, talk and behave—are a reflection of our relationship with God. If the inside is right, the outside will take care of itself. Moses did not know that his face was shining. That was not an act he was putting on to impress people. It was the natural consequence of his time with God.

The Pharisees were right on the outside but wrong on the inside.

Jesus said,

"Woe unto you, scribes and Pharisees, hypocrites! for ye make clean the outside of the cup and of the platter, but within they are full of extortion and excess.

"Thou blind Pharisee, cleanse first that which is within the cup and platter, that the outside of them may be clean also.

"Woe unto you, scribes and Pharisees, hypocrites! for ye are like unto whited sepulchres, which indeed appear beautiful outward, but are within full of dead men's bones, and of all uncleanness.

"Even so ye also outwardly appear righteous unto men, but within ye are full of hypocrisy and iniquity."—Matt. 23:25–28.

For those of us who believe and preach what God's Word says about outward appearance, there is a danger that we can fall into the trap of the Pharisees. They thought that as long as everything looked good on the outside, things were fine. However, no amount of outward compliance with rules can ever substitute for obedience in the heart.

In Psalm 51:6, David said, "Behold, thou desirest truth in the inward parts: and in the hidden part thou shalt make me to know wisdom." The sin of the Pharisees was hypocrisy—the inward and outward did not match.

There is also the danger that we can become judgmental. There are some good people in our city. They don't dress the way I believe the Bible says they should. Their outward appearance does not match the standards I think they should meet. Yet they genuinely love God, pray and strive to keep close to God.

It would be wrong for me to judge them based on their appearance. It would be wrong for me to feel more spiritual because I look different than they do. In fact, Paul said that when we compare ourselves to others, we are "not wise" (II Cor. 10:12).

The idea that a Christian must be right either on the inside *or* on the outside, and that he cannot be right both inwardly *and* outwardly simultaneously, is erroneous.

It is possible and necessary for us to be right both inwardly and outwardly. Make it your goal and purpose to be right both on the inside and on the outside. Since God looks on the heart, I need to have a right heart in order to please Him. Since man looks on the outward appearance, I need to have a good testimony in my appearance in order to draw men to God.

I heard about a young girl in our church who volunteered to help her mother with the dishes. As her mother watched, she saw that her daughter was washing only the inside of the cups. When the mother asked about that, the little girl said, "Well, Preacher said he'd rather have things clean on the inside!"

If I had to choose, that's the choice I would make; but it's far better to have the dishes clean inside *and* out! In our walk with God, we do not have to choose between inward and outward righteousness. He expects us to be right and do right and bring honor and glory to Him with our lives.

Chapter Ten

Was Jesus Born on December 25?

There are people to whom the celebration of Christmas, or not celebrating it, is a major issue. I don't believe this is the kind of issue over which people should break fellowship. It's not a fundamental of the faith. We ought to be able to get along with God's people unless there are substantive scriptural issues on which we cannot agree.

However, this is also not an issue on which we have to be confused. Careful study and comparing Scripture with Scripture allow us to arrive at a conclusion based, not on someone's opinions, but on the Word of God.

The Common Teaching

The common but incorrect teaching is that we can't really have any idea when Jesus was born, and sometimes there is a corollary teaching that Christians should not celebrate Christmas. The people who promote this belief say that December 25 is just adopted from a pagan holiday with a veneer of Christianity covering it. This common teaching may have some basis in historical fact.

In the fourth century, the Roman emperor Constantine was facing a large battle against rather significant odds. He claimed he had a vision and saw a cross. A voice said, "In the sign of this cross conquer." He went out and won the battle.

As a result, he made Christianity a legal religion in the empire; but most people believe it was not a genuine conversion. Since the pagan priests in their temples were looking at unemployment, they simply added a few rituals, changed a few names and called themselves Christians.

They gave Christian names to pagan practices. That is the true beginning of the Roman Catholic Church. It wasn't started by Peter. That is also the source of many of the errors of the Catholics. They worship Mary because pagan priests changed the names of their goddess and people followed right along.

Those who object to celebrating Christmas and declare that we do not know when Jesus was born typically teach the following.

Christmas trees and decorations are forbidden by Scripture.

People who object to Christmas trees most often refer to Jeremiah 10 for their proof text.

"For the customs of the people are vain: for one cutteth a tree out of the forest, the work of the hands of the workman, with the axe.

"They deck it with silver and with gold; they fasten it with nails and with hammers, that it move not."—Vss. 3, 4.

They say that this passage is referring to our custom of putting up and decorating Christmas trees. However, the verses surrounding verses 3 and 4, the context, are clearly talking about idols made from trees. The prophet says that since they cannot speak or move and have no power, there is no need to be afraid of false idols (vs. 5).

December 25 was celebrated as the Mithraic feast day.

Mithra was the Persian version of the Hindu sun god Mitra. According to the Zoroastrian religion, Mithra was the god of light, and his feast was celebrated each year on December 25.[1] At the time when Constantine made Christianity a legal religion in Rome, worship of Mithra was very widespread throughout the empire, particularly among the soldiers of the Roman army.

---

[1] However, celebration of this date did not begin until a decree by Aurelian in A.D. 274. As we will see, earlier Christian sources had already claimed December 25 as the date of Christ's birth. Others claim Christians chose the date to replace celebration of the Saturnalia. Actually, this celebration ran from December 17 to 23. If the purpose was to prevent this celebration, would they have chosen a date two days after it was over?

The Roman Catholic Church took the pagan Zoroastrian holiday and renamed it Christ's Mass.

The first recorded celebration of Christmas on December 25 in the Roman Empire took place in A.D. 336, twenty-three years after "Christianity" became a legal religion.[2] There is no question that some of the elements of early Christmas celebrations came from pagan religions.

This association led many Christians to frown on the celebration of Christmas. In fact, in the early days of the Massachusetts Bay Colony, a fine of five shillings was imposed on anyone found following the "popish tradition" of celebrating Christmas.

THE CONTRADICTORY TRUTH

Regarding the celebration of Christmas and the timing of Christ's birth, I believe there is much to be gained by studying history and Scripture. An honest conclusion from such study will be in contrast to what some teach.

The Christmas tree has a Christian origin.

In Dr. John R. Rice's sermon "Should a Christian Observe Christmas?" which is in the book *Great Preaching on Christmas,* he recounts the story of the origin of the Christmas tree.

In the eighth century, a missionary named Boniface went to Germany to preach Christ. The Germanic tribes worshiped the oak tree. They thought of it as a symbol of deity. Boniface told them the oak tree was a poor symbol for God. It sheds its leaves and appears to die each winter. The tree that should remind them of God, he said, was the evergreen. It is always green and thriving.

Christmas trees became popular in England primarily through the influence of the German-born Prince Albert, husband of England's Queen Victoria. In America they were introduced by the Dutch (German) immigrants to Pennsylvania. Because the Christmas tree has a Christian origin and is not forbidden in

---

[2] The Encyclopedia Britannica states that Sextus Julius Africanus identified December 25 as the date of Christ's birth in A.D. 221. Also, many manuscripts of Hippolytus' commentary on Daniel (vol. 2, sec. 4) give December 25 as the date; Hippolytus died in A.D. 236. According to the *International book of Christmas Carols,* around A.D. 130, Telesphorus instituted public church services to celebrate the nativity, while at the same time, Theophilus was urging the celebratin of Christ's birth on December 25. All of these predate Aurelian's decree to celebrate Mithra on that day. Given Aurelian's animosity to Christianity, perhaps *he* was the one trying to take over a holiday!

Scripture, there is no reason to preach against it and cut people off from what can be a very enjoyable and memorable part of celebrating the birth of Christ.

The Bible does not rule out December as the month when Christ was born.

It is true that Scripture does not give us an exact date for the birth of Christ. However, through careful study we can demonstrate that Jesus could indeed have been born very close to the traditional date of December 25.

a) The Hebrew religious year begins with the month Nisan.

The Hebrew calendar has 354 days instead of 365 days, so their calendar does not exactly line up with the one we use. The Hebrew month Nisan roughly corresponds with mid-March to mid-April on our calendar. In this month they celebrate the Passover and Israel's deliverance from Egypt. The first month of the Hebrew religious year is the month Nisan.

b) The priests who served in the temple served after a pattern established by King David.

According to I Chronicles 24, the descendants of Aaron were divided by David into twenty-four groups to serve two roles—as governors of the sanctuary and governors of the house of God (I Chron. 24:5). Each group of priests served according to a schedule drawn up by the casting of lots (vss. 7–18).

It would seem from II Chronicles 23:8 that the priests served for a week a a time. This meant that each group knew when they were due to leave their homes and go to Jerusalem for their time of service Each would serve twice a year, along with the mandatory feasts of Passover, Firstfruits and Tabernacles, when all the priests served. This would complete the entire year in their calendar.

c) Zacharias, the father of John the Baptist, served in the eighth course.

Luke 1:5 says, "There was in the days of Herod, the king of Judæa, a certain priest named Zacharias, of the course of Abia [Abijah]: and his wife was of the daughters of Aaron, and her name was Elisabeth."

According to I Chronicles 24:10, the family of Abijah was assigned the eighth course. That meant that Abijah and his descendants after him would fulfill their duty to serve in the eighth and thirty-second turns. Because of how the feasts fell, this would be the ninth and thirty-fifth weeks of the year.

As a descendant of Abijah, Zacharias would have served in the temple in these two weeks of the Hebrew calendar. They would fall in the spring and autumn on our calendar. Zacharias was fulfilling his normal term of service when the angel Gabriel appeared and told him he and Elisabeth were going to have a son.

d) If this was the second rotation for the year, Zacharias would have completed his service and gone home in the fall.

The Bible tells us that Zacharias stayed and completed his normal duties in the temple before returning home (Luke 1:23). It was probably shortly after his return that Elisabeth conceived, as promised by the angel. The date for the conception of John the Baptist in this case would be the end of October.

We are told that Elisabeth hid herself five months after conceiving John (vs. 24).

e) Gabriel appeared to Mary in the sixth month of Elisabeth's pregnancy to announce the birth of Christ.

The start of the sixth month of Elisabeth's pregnancy would have probably been early spring. It was at that time that Gabriel announced to Mary that she would be the mother of the Messiah. He also told her that her cousin Elisabeth was pregnant (vss. 26–36).

f) Normal gestation for a human baby is nine months.

If the angel Gabriel made his announcement to Mary sometime in the early spring, nine months from then would be early winter. We do not know for certain that Jesus was born on December 25, but a careful study of Scripture gives us good reason to believe that it could have been very close to that date.

g) The shepherds were in the field.

Some have objected that shepherds would not have been in the fields at night in December. However, there was a field between Bethlehem and Jerusalem which was the location of the "tower of the flock" mentioned in Micha 4:8. Shepherds kept the spotless lambs chosen for temple sacrifice there year round. Since the verse comes just seven verses before the great Messianic prophecy of Christ's birth in Micha 5:2, some believe this to be a prophecy of where the announcement was to be made, and that these special shepherds were the ones who heard the angels.

We have seen two separate verifications from the scriptural chronology and the testimony of history that Jesus could have been born around Christmastime. There are some people who honestly object to celebrating Christmas, but it is not legitimate for them to do so on the basis that Jesus could not have been born at that time.[3]

Certainly there are things associated with Christmas, especially here in America, that are of concern to all of us. Santa Claus is a fictional character about whom I believe you ought to tell your kids the truth. Don't teach your children Santa Claus brings them presents. Why would you want some stranger to get the credit when you are the one who spends all the money? I never have understood that.

It's dangerous to build up falsehoods. If you lie to them about Santa Claus, eventually they'll wonder if you lied to them about other things as well.

The excessive materialism of our culture can easily overwhelm the meaning of Christmas; but if things are kept in their proper perspective, there is absolutely nothing wrong with celebrating the birth of Christ.

Thε Consεquεncεs Taught

Understanding the truth about the birth of Christ from a careful study of the Word of God rather than accepting the traditions of what others say is important. From such study we not only learn the truth about Christmas, but we also learn much about the Bible and how God works as well.

The Bible adds up.

It's fascinating to me that I can take what the Bible gives me and arrive at a logical conclusion. Even if people hadn't been celebrating Christ's birth on December 25 for centuries, we would still have the shepherds in the fields with their lambs and the calendar cal-

---

[3] No less an authority than Alfred Edersheim said, "There is no adequate reason for questioning the historical accuracy of [December 25]. The objections generally made rest on grounds, which seem to me historically untenable." (*The Life and Times of Jesus the Messiah*, book 2, chapter 6.)

culations from Zacharias that would establish that as the time of year Christ was born.

You could study the Bible for ten hours a day for the rest of your life and never run out of things to learn. God has given us a wonderful Book. If you find something that doesn't seem to add up, it's your adding, not the Bible's numbers, that is at fault.

If you don't see how something in the Bible could be true, don't assume that the Bible is wrong—it isn't. Be patient and be attentive. Eventually somebody will figure it out.

Skeptics used to criticize the Bible account of the birth of Christ because Luke talked about its being "when Cyrenius was governor of Syria." They said Cyrenius wasn't governor until years later. Then when they dug a little deeper into the archaeological record, they found that twice Cyrenius had been governor of Syria. The first time he was governor was when Christ was born, and the second time was later. I have yet to see any published articles in any of the national news journals admitting that the skeptics were wrong and the Bible had been proven right; but the Bible record stands every test and challenge.

People used to criticize the Bible because there was no evidence of the race called the Hittites. Through the years the archaeologists continued digging. Ultimately, they found ample proof of the existence of the Hittites. Given enough time, the scientific investigators will usually catch up with the Bible.

The Bible has much more to tell us than we have learned.

Have you ever thought this way? *I've read the Bible so much, there's nothing new for me to learn.* That's wrong. I had a man tell me once, "I've been in church so long, there's no sermon I haven't heard. I've heard all the sermons there are to preach." I said to him, "I haven't even heard all of my sermons yet."

We always have more to learn. I read the Bible through several times each year. Every two months, I read through the New Testament. Every three months, I read through the Old Testament. I do not discover deep and wonderful truths every day, but I'm always seeing things I had not seen before.

For example, I preached a sermon once about Phinehas. He was

Aaron's grandson who stopped a plague by killing the Israelite who brought a Midianite woman into his tent (Num. 25:6–8). I mentioned in passing in the message that later on in his life Phinehas made it into the Promised Land (Josh. 22:13). Someone came up to me after church and said that he must have been under twenty because all the men twenty years old and up died in the wilderness except Caleb and Joshua.

I read more carefully and found that the death penalty pronounced on all the men twenty years and older did not apply to the Levites. They were not counted when the people were numbered (Num. 26:62, 63). The Levites all got to go to the Promised Land, regardless of their age. It was there all the time in the Word of God. I just hadn't seen it before.

The Bible, therefore, is worthy of our careful study.

I believe you should read the Bible like a person who is mining for gold. I have a chunk of gold ore in my office that somebody gave me. Everything in that rock that looks like gold isn't gold. The sparkly stuff is fool's gold. The real gold looks more like rust. It would take fifteen tons of ore like the rock I have to get one ounce of pure gold.

When you read the Bible for your personal devotions, look for gold. Don't try to examine every rock. Don't try to pulverize it and do a chemical analysis. Just look till you find some gold. Look for nuggets. Don't get stuck on something that you don't fully understand.

H. A. Ironside was once asked, "What do you do with all the hard parts in the Bible?" He said, "I do the same thing I do when I'm eating fish. I put the bones on the side of the plate for someone else to choke on, and I eat the rest of the fish."

When I'm having devotions, I don't try to do in-depth analysis, but there should be times when we study in depth. When something arrests our attention, we should make a note of it so we can follow it up at a later time. We should study the Bible, just as we did with finding the time line for the birth of Christ, until we come up with the answer. We'll find fascinating and amazing truths as we carefully study the Word of God.

God's timing is perfect.

Isn't it interesting that the Lamb of God who came to take away

100

the sins of the world (John 1:29) was born at the same time the lambs out in the field were being born? Paul said that Jesus was born "when the fulness of the time was come" (Gal. 4:4). God never does anything accidentally.

Bethlehem is only a few miles from Jerusalem. It's very possible that the shepherds to whom the angel announced the birth of Christ were the same shepherds who kept the sheep for the temple to provide the lambs for the sacrifices. The symbolism associated with the birth of Christ is very powerful.

We can always count on God to work at exactly the right time in exactly the right way. One of the things that careful study of God's Word does for us is to build our faith by showing us how God makes "every thing beautiful in his time" (Eccles. 3:11).

CHAPTER ELEVEN

MAY WE DEFEND OURSELVES, OR MUST WE ALWAYS TURN THE OTHER CHEEK?

Of all the things that Jesus taught, there are probably as much confusion and disagreement about 'turning the other cheek' as there are about anything else. Lester Roloff, who was known for being somewhat pugnacious, said, "The reason you turn the other cheek is to set up a full roundhouse swing!" Some people believe that Jesus was teaching against self-defense in this passage. Others take this to mean that Jesus was teaching a complete pacifism. Let's look first at how the doctrine of turning the other cheek is commonly interpreted.

COMMON TEACHING

It is commonly taught that Jesus commanded Christians to turn the other cheek.

In Matthew 5:39, Jesus said, "But I say unto you, That ye resist not evil: but whosoever shall smite thee on thy right cheek, turn to him the other also." There is no question that Jesus did command His followers to 'turn the other cheek.'

Jesus never defended Himself.

"And the chief priests accused him of many things: but he answered nothing.

"And Pilate asked him again, saying, Answerest thou nothing? behold how many things they witness against thee.

"But Jesus yet answered nothing; so that Pilate marvelled."—Mark 15:3–5.

103

Even in the face of false accusations brought against Him by witnesses who had been hired to lie about Him, Jesus was silent. He was given opportunities to defend Himself against their lies, but He refused. He did not use His divine power to destroy the soldiers who arrested Him. Instead, He allowed Himself to be put to death when a single word would have stopped the whole process.

Christians who want to follow Jesus' example should not defend themselves.

What would Jesus do? This question, taken from the book *In His Steps* by Charles M. Sheldon, has become popular today. You can find it on T-shirts, backpacks, book covers and even on bracelets. I believe this is sometimes done out of context, but certainly it is good to act in the same way that Jesus would.

Since Jesus refused to fight back and defend Himself when He could have, those who hold to this belief say that we should do the same. They state that if we defend ourselves, we are not following Christ's example. They teach a doctrine of pacifism. Some denominations, such as the Quakers, believe it's wrong ever to use force, no matter what the situation or circumstance.

It is wrong for Christians to use force to defend themselves or others.

Not everyone who holds the belief that we should not defend ourselves because of Jesus' teaching goes this far, but some people actually argue that we should not use force to defend others either. Their contention is that the use of force is always wrong under any set of circumstances.

It is wrong for a Christian to serve in the military.

Some people think there is no justification for war or fighting. They believe that Christians should not be a part of the armed forces or fight for their country. There are some problems with this approach, not the least of which is that we live in a wicked and sinful world. If people know they can take advantage of you and you won't defend yourself, such people will probably take advantage of you. My father told me once, "There are some people who don't understand anything except a good swift kick in the seat of the pants." Regardless of that reality, there are still people who oppose Christians involved in the military.

THE CONTRADICTORY TRUTH

Jesus did, on many occasions, answer His critics.

I knew a man once who was fond of saying, "Never explain and never complain." A pastor who was well known across the country said, "I'll never defend myself. People can say whatever they want to about me, but I'll keep silent." There are times when it is wiser to hold your peace than to answer your critics. Sometimes you need to trust the Lord to take care of you without your saying or doing anything by way of self-defense.

However, the Bible also says, "A good name is rather to be chosen than great riches" (Prov. 22:1). It should be your goal to have people think of you as honorable and honest and upright because you do what you are supposed to do. If someone says something seriously critical about my character, I'll call and confront him about it.

Over the years I've found that the people who criticize you to others are usually embarrassed to say anything to you directly. They don't seem to mind talking *about* you, but when it comes to talking *to* you, that's a little more difficult for them.

One time a man consented to allow a paper to interview him. He made some comments that they published which I thought were directed at me. He didn't name me in the interview, but he described a set of circumstances that sounded like he was talking about me. Among other things, he said, "The way to keep from changing your convictions is to keep associating with the same people. I know a man who used to associate with a certain preacher, and now he doesn't. He's changed."

I called him up and asked him if he had been talking about me. He replied that he had. I said, "I hope you're a good enough friend that you'll tell me how I've changed. As far as I know, I haven't changed. I still use the same Bible. I still go soul winning. I haven't lowered the standards at our church."

He said, "You don't go to this meeting anymore. You don't speak for this preacher anymore."

I said, "That's true, but you were talking about a person's changing his convictions. Mine are still the same, even though I don't associate with that man any longer." He apologized and said he

105

hadn't chosen his words as wisely as he could have.

I think facing him about the matter was the right thing to do. I didn't attack him, but I did outline my position.

"And it came to pass, as Jesus sat at meat in the house, behold, many publicans and sinners came and sat down with him and his disciples.

"And when the Pharisees saw it, they said unto his disciples, Why eateth your Master with publicans and sinners?

"But when Jesus heard that, he said unto them, They that be whole need not a physician, but they that are sick.

"But go ye and learn what that meaneth, I will have mercy, and not sacrifice: for I am not come to call the righteous, but sinners to repentance."—Matt. 9:10–13.

When the Pharisees criticized Jesus for spending time with sinners, He explained His purpose and motivation to them. Reaching sinners was the purpose for His coming into the world. The point is that Jesus did not allow their criticism to go unanswered. This was hardly the only instance in which He refused to allow people to say false, harmful and untrue things about Him.

Jesus instructed the disciples to prepare to defend themselves.

"Then said he unto them, But now, he that hath a purse, let him take it, and likewise his script: and he that hath no sword, let him sell his garment, and buy one.

"For I say unto you, that this that is written must yet be accomplished in me, And he was reckoned among the transgressors: for the things concerning me have an end.

"And they said, Lord, behold, here are two swords. And he said unto them, It is enough."—Luke 22:36–38.

Jesus specifically told His disciples to arm themselves. In fact, He placed such a level of importance on this instruction that He told them, if necessary, to sell their garment to buy a sword. People didn't have a large variety of clothing in Bible days. Jesus was not telling them to have a yard sale and get rid of castoff clothing. He was emphasizing the great coming need for protection.

God commanded His people to go to war.

"Samuel also said unto Saul, The LORD sent me to anoint thee to be king over his people, over Israel: now therefore hearken thou unto the voice of the words of the LORD.

"Thus saith the LORD of hosts, I remember that which Amalek did to Israel, how he laid wait for him in the way, when he came up from Egypt.

"Now go and smite Amalek, and utterly destroy all that they have, and spare them not; but slay both man and woman, infant and suckling, ox and sheep, camel and ass."—I Sam. 15:1–3.

You cannot read the Bible honestly and come to the conclusion that God always disapproves of war for any reason. He commanded war. You cannot be a pacifist and believe the Bible unless you misinterpret Scripture. The war God commanded against the Amalekites was not defensive. It was retributive. God was judging Amalek for what they had done in the past. This was an offensive war. God commanded His people to execute the utter destruction of the Amalekites.

Jesus did *not* say, "Smite thee on thy cheek."

Jesus specifically talked about someone being smitten on the right cheek. It's important that we take the Bible for exactly what it says. If the point was to turn the other cheek whenever someone hit you, why would Jesus mention the right cheek? The Lord was not just throwing in useless information. That qualifier is in the verse for a reason.

Being smitten on the right cheek was done with the back of the hand.

A right-handed person, which between 85 and 90 percent of people are, hitting someone on the cheek, would normally hit him on the left cheek. If two people were standing facing each other, the only way for one of them to smite the right cheek of the other would be with the back of the hand.

Jewish law taught that it was a double insult to strike someone with the back of the hand rather than with the palm.

In his book *Cowboy Boots in Darkest Africa,* Dr. Bill Rice told the story of meeting a group of seven warriors on his missionary trip to Africa. What he did not know until later was that those men had just killed a group of Dutch workers. As they approached him, the leader tried to stab Dr. Rice with his spear, but it caught on his belt buckle. Dr. Rice reacted by slapping him with the back of his hand, and the warriors immediately retreated.

He said that it must have been God's leading for him to slap the man. In their tribal culture, the way a chief rebuked a warrior was with a back hand slap. Seeing Dr. Rice respond in that way, the men were sure he was a great leader and left him alone.

When Jesus said, 'Turn the other cheek,' He was not talking about responding to an injury. He was not saying it is wrong to defend yourself against an attack. He was not saying you must accept an injury without reacting. What He was saying is that you do not have to respond to an insult.

If you are attacked, you have every right to defend yourself. You have not just a right but an obligation to defend your family from physical danger. Jesus told the disciples to buy swords in order to be prepared to defend themselves.

In our country, the Second Amendment to the Constitution guarantees us the right to own weapons. About two million times a year, citizens in the United States use a gun to defend themselves. When they do so, they have fewer unjustified shootings than do the police when they use their weapons. Every state that allows carrying concealed weapons has seen a decrease in the rate of violent crimes. It is right and proper to defend your country, your family and your home.

CONSEQUENCES TAUGHT

It is right to protect yourself and others from physical attack.

There may be occasions when it is wise to allow yourself to suffer an injury without retaliating. When I was an assistant pastor years ago, the former pastor of the church was visiting a home, and the man to whom he was talking punched him in the face. The pastor didn't say anything or fight back; instead, he just left the house. The man was bragging around town about having beaten up the preacher. Someone heard him talking and said, "That man is a

Golden Gloves boxing champion. He could have knocked you out cold. He just chose not to!" I believe that was the right choice for that pastor.

While there may be times when you choose not to defend yourself, it is also right to protect yourself and others from physical attacks.

It is right to correct wrong statements made by your adversaries.

I'm not talking about being hypersensitive and responding to every person who even looks at you cross-eyed. Many things are not worthy of a response. However, if someone attacks your character or falsely accuses you of some moral failing, it's both right and appropriate for you to respond. This is the pattern Jesus established with the Pharisees. He did not attack them in return, but He did explain the true motives for His behavior.

Facts are a powerful response to falsehoods to people who care about the truth. Some people do not, and answering them is generally unproductive; but someone who wants to know the truth deserves a calm explanation of the facts.

It is wrong to fight back out of fleshly motives or a desire for vengeance.

There is no Bible justification for "getting even." If your purpose is to correct false statements made about you and thereby protect your good name, it is proper to respond. If your purpose is to try to seek retribution against someone who said something about you, that is wrong.

The Bible teaches us that vengeance belongs to God (Rom. 12:19). You can and should trust God to execute justice on those who mistreat you. The fact that you have the right to respond does not give you the right to take justice into your own hands.

It is right to try to maintain a good name.

We've already seen in Proverbs 22:1 the value that God places on having a good name. Shakespeare put it this way in *Othello:*

Good name in man and woman, dear my lord,
Is the immediate jewel of their souls:
Who steals my purse steals trash; 'tis something, nothing;
'Twas mine, 'tis his and has been slave to thousands;
But he that filches from me my good name

109

**Robs me of that which not enriches him
And makes me poor indeed.**

You should work to make sure that your own actions and words always are a credit to your Christian testimony. Your reputation is a valuable asset, and it is worthy of protection.

It is essential to learn the discipline and the power of restraint.

Jesus was saying not to fight back even when it lies within your power to do so. When you are mocked or called names or made fun of, you can take it in silence. Let those hurling the insults do it again if they want to. The truth is that most of us are more worried about being insulted than we are about being injured. That's why we need this lesson!

When I was about twelve, I watched as a little boy who was probably eight or nine tried to get money from my father. He said, "If you don't give me a dime, I'm going to punch you in the stomach." My dad looked at him and said, "You won't do that." The little boy said, "Why not?" Dad replied, "Because if you do, I'll step on your foot." The boy walked away. Dad was exercising restraint. It takes more grace to do that than it does to fight back.

The sad truth is that we rarely get upset when the name of Christ is harmed. We seldom react strongly when the work of God is damaged. Most of the time when we get upset, it's about an insult to us. Our focus is in the wrong place.

First Baptist Church of Bridgeport had its first meeting in 1950. The church was officially organized in 1952. The early members completed their first building in 1963. That little building is still there on Sun Valley Road. From what I've read in the records of the church, they started meeting there before the heating system was hooked up. People brought in charcoal grills to warm up the building.

Most of the work had been done by the members. The pastor stood up in the first service and began thanking people who had worked on the project. There was one man, a builder by trade, who had done more than anyone else to get the building done. The only name the preacher forgot to call out was his. That man said, "That's it. I did all that work and put in all that time. He doesn't appreciate what I did. I'll never go back to his church again." As far as I know, he never did. He wasn't injured; he was just insulted.

It is Christlike to be willing to be insulted in order to maintain a good testimony.

I've known people who got angry when they were falsely attacked. Then they decided to defend themselves and lost control. Even though they were innocent of what was said about them originally, they damaged their testimony by what they said and did. I've been embarrassed for people arguing with great intensity over trivial things. It is possible to do yourself more harm than good in your attempt at self-defense.

The Lord wasn't saying not to defend yourself when He said, 'Turn the other cheek.' He wasn't saying not to deal with a matter that questions or puts a blight on your character. He was saying if people insult you, don't respond. Let them say it again and again if they want to. You always have the choice just to let it go. You can trust God to take care of it for you.

CHAPTER TWELVE
IS THERE A DIFFERENCE BETWEEN BIG SINS AND LITTLE SINS?

All my life in many different churches, I've heard people say, "There are no big sins or little sins. It's all sin with God." I heard about a man who was called to serve on a jury. The case under consideration involved a marijuana possession charge. The defense attorney, in questioning the prospective jurors, asked this man whether he made a distinction between large offenses and small offenses. The man replied, "I believe that if you borrow a penny, you're in debt." He was excused from serving on the jury. The lawyer didn't want someone on the jury who believed there was no difference!

I believe that the motivation of most of the people who teach that there is no difference between big sins and little sins is good. I think their purpose is to encourage people to do right. The question is, Does that concept match up with what the Bible says?

THE COMMON TEACHING

It is commonly taught that there are no big sins or little sins.

The proponents of this doctrine say that the Bible does not make any distinction between big sins and little sins. They point to the fact that God's Word condemns sin broadly, never making exception for "little white lies" or other things that society tolerates. I believe it is admirable for these people not to try to make excuses for sin nor to find ways to excuse small sins.

All sins are equal in God's eyes.

In Matthew 5:21, 22, Jesus said,

113

"Ye have heard that it was said by them of old time, Thou shalt not kill; and whosoever shall kill shall be in danger of the judgment:

"But I say unto you, That whosoever is angry with his brother without a cause shall be in danger of the judgment: and whosoever shall say to his brother, Raca, shall be in danger of the council: but whosoever shall say, Thou fool, shall be in danger of hell fire."

Those who say there is no difference between big sins and little sins say these verses teach that Jesus said it was the same to be angry without cause as to murder. If you break the law in one point, you are guilty of all (Jas. 2:10).

My sin, therefore, is no worse than your sin.

I heard a man say, "Your judgmental attitude is just as bad in God's eyes as my looking at pornography." I counseled a man once who was upset because he was not allowed by the church he attended to teach Sunday school or be a deacon because he smoked. He said, "Everybody has sins. My sin is just in my pocket." He didn't see why that one visible sin should keep him from holding a leadership position in the church.

The danger with this concept is that it is easy to rationalize your own faults by comparing them to those of others. You can justify sin by finding someone else who is doing something similar. When I was in college, one of my friends transferred from Bob Jones to what was then known as Lynchburg Baptist College, now Liberty University.

My friend was a gifted piano player and began accompanying one of their singing groups. I found out they were going to be performing nearby, and several of us went to hear them. The music they performed wasn't quite the same as what I was used to hearing. It didn't quite line up with my standards; but one of my friends named a famous preacher we all like and respected and then said, "He uses those same songs. We shouldn't be critical when someone else does them." If a good person does something that I think is wrong, does that make it right?

Nobody is perfect. We're all going to get to Heaven and find out there were some things we did that were wrong that we didn't know were wrong. That's what the psalmist is talking about in Psalm 19 when he refers to "secret faults."

I sometimes am asked to preach in one church where ladies almost look Amish. They wear their dresses really long and don't wear makeup. I'm certainly not against having dress standards, even if they're stricter than mine; but in the same church, there were guys singing in the choir who were wearing blue jeans and T-shirts. That seems strange to me.

If I take the philosophy that something is all right because some famous Christian does it, I can justify almost anything. G. Campbell Morgan, the famous Bible commentator, drank brandy. Charles Spurgeon, the prince of preachers, smoked cigars. D. L. Moody was so overweight that he would literally rest his stomach on the pulpit while he preached.

If you follow that philosophy to its conclusion, you become a combination of the worst traits of the best people who've ever lived. Deny the Lord like Peter. Commit murder and adultery like David. Get angry and kill a man and bury him in the sand like Moses. Take a vow after preaching against it, like Paul did.

You never aid your Christian walk by imitating the faults of others. You should never let someone else's sin become the excuse or justification for your sin.

THE CONTRADICTORY TRUTH

There are *no* acceptable sins.

I think that some of the people who promote the common teaching are trying to get across the point that there is nothing that is acceptable to God that is a sin. On that point I would agree with them. There are no sins about which God says, "Oh, don't worry about that. It's no big deal."

Have you ever known anyone who was stopped by a police officer for going five miles an hour over the speed limit but was let off with a warning? In essence, a police officer who issues a warning is not fully enforcing the law. Sometimes the police are not terribly strict about the letter of the law.

I got too much change at a store one time, and as soon as I figured it out, I went back to return it. The man said, "It's my mistake, you can keep it." He was saying it was no big deal. God never says that about sin.

The Bible says, "For whosoever shall keep the whole law, and yet offend in one point, he is guilty of all" (Jas. 2:10). Does that mean if you've ever told a lie you might as well kill someone? Does that mean that if you've ever disobeyed your parents you might as well commit adultery? Does that mean that if you've ever gossiped you might as well steal? Of course not.

Think of the Ten Commandments. Think of them as ten links in a chain. Think of yourself hanging over Hell suspended from that chain. How many links do you have to break to fall? Just one. Once you have broken the law, you are a lawbreaker. Once you are a lawbreaker, you are ineligible for Heaven through your own works. That is the point James was making. No matter which sins you have avoided, if you've committed *any,* you're in trouble with God.

All sin grieves and displeases God.

Psalm 66:18 says, "If I regard iniquity in my heart, the Lord will not hear me." Sin has a definite impact on your relationship with God.

My friend Dr. Curtis Hutson said that his niece had been killed in an automobile accident. Dr. Hutson had conducted the funeral and had tried to comfort the family. A few years later, at a family gathering, Dr. Hutson and his relatives were watching old home movies that had his niece in them. After a few moments, his brother and sister-in-law went outside and started crying.

Dr. Hutson went outside and apologized to them for bringing up painful memories. They told him not to be sorry. His brother said, "It just hurts so bad." Dr. Hutson said, as he walked back inside, he thought of the verse "Grieve not the holy Spirit of God" (Eph. 4:30). He said, "Can I do something that makes God feel like that?" When we sin, it hurts the heart of God.

Different sins have different consequences.

"For it is the life of all flesh; the blood of it is for the life thereof: therefore I said unto the children of Israel, Ye shall eat the blood of no manner of flesh: for the life of all flesh is the blood thereof: whosoever eateth it shall be cut off.

"And every soul that eateth that which died of itself, or that which was torn with beasts, whether it be one of your own country, or a stranger, he shall both wash his clothes, and bathe himself in water, and be unclean until the even: then shall he be clean."—Lev. 17:14, 15.

Under the Mosaic Law, there was a distinction between a person's eating the blood of an animal that he killed and eating something that died on its own. For eating the blood of an animal he killed, a person was cut off; while for eating something that died a natural death, he was simply unclean.

"Men do not despise a thief, if he steal to satisfy his soul when he is hungry;

"But if he be found, he shall restore sevenfold; he shall give all the substance of his house.

"But whoso committeth adultery with a woman lacketh understanding: he that doeth it destroyeth his own soul.

"A wound and dishonour shall he get; and his reproach shall not be wiped away.

"For jealousy is the rage of a man: therefore he will not spare in the day of vengeance.

"He will not regard any ransom; neither will he rest content, though thou givest many gifts."—Prov. 6:30–35.

Having to repay seven times what one stole is a pretty stiff penalty, but is doesn't begin to compare to the penalty for adultery. An adulterer has destroyed his own soul. There is no other sin in the Bible of which God says that the reproach never goes away. That doesn't mean that an adulterer can't be forgiven, but there is a stigma that comes with adultery that does not come with other sins.

"Who can understand his errors? cleanse thou me from secret faults.

"Keep back thy servant also from presumptuous sins; let them not have dominion over me: then shall I be upright, and I shall be innocent from the great transgression."—Ps. 19:12, 13.

I was intrigued by the distinction among errors, presumptuous sins and secret faults.

According to this passage, there are some things that are larger transgressions than others. There are sins that we commit that we don't even know about. Presumptuous sins are those where we knowingly choose to do wrong. If we purposefully sin, sin gains dominion over us. We start out the master and end up the slave.

While there are no good, acceptable, okay or irrelevant sins, there are some sins that have greater consequences and repercussions than other sins have. That's a plain truth taught repeatedly throughout Scripture.

117

Once a preacher objected to my having invited a certain man to preach at our church. It wasn't really any of his business whom we had preach at our church, but he was trying to convince me I was wrong to have this man in our pulpit. He felt this person I had invited had been dishonest. I said, "I've known some preachers who have exaggerated." Anybody who's spoken much has said a few things that didn't come out quite right.

I think the man I invited did stretch the truth once in a while. I heard him say once, "The basic facts of the story are correct." He embellished his stories a little sometimes. I think dishonesty is a terrible thing, and I don't want to be dishonest; but if every preacher who exaggerated a single story had to leave the ministry, there would be an awful lot of empty pulpits on Sunday morning.

You ought to be on guard against all sins, but it's most important to beware of presumptuous sins because they lead to great transgressions. Something you know is wrong but you think you can handle is the most dangerous sin of all.

THE CONSEQUENCES OF THE TRUTH

No sin is good, but some sins are worse than others.

In George Orwell's classic parable about communism, *Animal Farm,* the animals run the oppressive farmer off and take over the operation of the farm themselves. At the beginning of their rule, they post several guiding principles on the side of the barn. The very first principle is "All animals are equal."

Over the course of the story, the pigs rise to a leadership position at the farm and begin living off the work of the other animals. As time passes, they changed the rules to benefit themselves. Finally, the first principle is rewritten to read, "All animals are equal, but some animals are more equal than others."

Clearly it is worse to drive 150 miles per hour than it is to double park. Both are against the law. A policeman can write tickets for both offenses, but they won't be for the same amount.

**Never excuse your sin by comparing it
to the sin of another.**

When I was just a young preacher, I was talking to an older preacher about preachers and sin. He said, "You hear about these guys messing up and committing adultery. For every one who commits adultery, there are ten who compromise; and for every ten who compromise, there are a hundred who are proud. The compromising preachers and the proud preachers do far more harm to the cause of Christ than one preacher who commits adultery. Remember David was called a man after God's own heart before and after his sin."

The problem is, that's not true. As we've already seen, the Bible clearly teaches that adultery has greater consequences than other sins. The only time David was called a man after God's own heart was **before** he was anointed king by Samuel (I Sam. 13:14 and quoted in the New Testament in Acts 13:22). It's never said about David *after* his sin with Bathsheba.

Some years later, I was preaching in another state, and there was a lady on staff at the church where I was speaking with whom I had worked with when I was a teenager. After I preached, she came up and asked if she could talk to me confidentially. When her story unfolded, I found out that she was involved in an immoral relationship with that same pastor who had downplayed the seriousness of preachers' committing adultery.

As I thought about what that man had said, I realized that perhaps he had been attempting to downplay his own sin. He liked to quote Martin Luther as having said that it was good for great Christians to have some sin in their lives so they could experience God's grace. I don't know if Martin Luther ever said that or not, but I know what Paul said: "Shall we continue in sin, that grace may abound? God forbid"! (Rom. 6:1, 2). The Bible trumps Martin Luther every time.

Little sins can lead to big sins.

The psalmist warned that presumptuous sins lead to the great transgressions. If we tolerate "little sins," we are placing ourselves in grave danger.

For many years, the greatest animal trainer in the world was Gunther Gebel-Williams. He was so outstanding that the Ringling Brothers and Barnum and Bailey Circus purchased the entire European circus company for which he worked so they could add him to their show.

He was known as the "Lord of the Rings," and his flamboyant

smile never faltered whether he was working with horses, elephants, tigers or lions. His amazing act was the highlight of the circus for more than twenty years.

In an interview not long before he retired, Williams stated that he was quitting in part because he had become too accustomed to the big cats that were the centerpiece of his act. He felt that he had lost some of his fear of them—and recognized the danger in that loss.

Sin is not to be played with. The Devil is just looking for an opportunity to devour you and destroy your life.

Imitating the flaws of greatly used Christians will only make you worse.

Smoking cigars wouldn't make me preach more like Spurgeon. Drinking brandy wouldn't make me an expositor like Morgan. Weighing 350 pounds wouldn't make me a great evangelist like Moody. Rather than imitating the faults of others, we need to imitate their virtues.

Dr. Frank Garlock told of a famous conductor under whom he once studied. The man was frustrated that his students weren't learning the important lessons he was trying to teach. He said, "How I talk and how I spit—this they copy."

It's important to your spiritual health and your relationship with God that you maintain the proper attitude toward sin. Don't ever excuse a sin because someone you respect allows it. Don't tolerate anything remaining in your life that you know to be wrong. Don't make the mistake of forgetting that the Devil wants to destroy you. Remain committed to doing right, and your life will be pleasing to God.

For a complete list of books available from the Sword of the Lord, write to Sword of the Lord Publishers, P. O. Box 1099, Murfreesboro, Tennessee 37133.

(800) 251-4100
(615) 893-6700
FAX (615) 848-6943
www.swordofthelord.com